An Authentic Woman

Soulwork for the Wisdom Years

BettyClare Moffatt

A Fireside Book
Published by Simon & Schuster

F

FIRESIDE
Rockefeller Center
1230 Avenue of the Americas
New York, NY 10020

FIRESIDE and colophon are registered trademarks
of Simon & Schuster Inc.

Designed by Judy Wong

Manufactured in the United States of America

3   5   7   9   10   8   6   4   2

Library of Congress Cataloging-in-Publication Data
Moffatt, BettyClare.
An authentic woman: soulwork for the wisdom
years/ BettyClare Moffatt.
p.   cm.
1. Middle aged women—Religious life.   2. Aged women—
Religious life.   3. Spiritual life.   I. Title.
BL625.3.M64   1999
158′.082—dc21   98-49912   CIP
ISBN 0-684-84444-3

To Nancy Love, dear friend and esteemed agent.
When I first met you, I vowed that I would sell
all my books through Love. And so it is. In gratitude for
believing in the vision and the power of the words.

Contents

Contents

Contents

Mature Authenticity

Story-Telling Women

The best thing you can have in life is to have someone tell you a story.

LESLIE MARMON SILKO

Tell me a story, dear friend. Tell me how you grew into the woman that you are. Tell me how you coped with poverty and illness and pain and grew into the strength you are to others. Tell me how you manage to be wry, witty, ironic; tell me how you keep your sense of humor. Tell me how you could care for, and then bury, husband, child, mother, father, and walk away intact.

I want to know your hopes and dreams and wishes, dear friend. Tell me how you reconcile desire with the reality of an aging body. Tell me how you blossom in self-esteem as the world ignores you. Tell me how you start over again and again, rise like a phoenix from the ashes, resurrect yourself, and go forward.

Tell me a story, dear friend. Tell me of your core self, your inner spiritual quest, your divine feminine soul that guides you onward.

Tell me how you wake each day with new perceptions, new eyes to see the stories all around you. Tell me of your curiosity, your zest for life. Tell me of your creativity. Tell me how you have learned to blend love and work, love and wisdom, love and loss, love and new beginnings.

Then tell me how you continue. Tell me how you redefine, reshape, remold, renew, restore, and regenerate yourself. Tell me what you give to others, and how you have learned to give to yourself. Tell me what you have received from others and how you are a blessing.

Share your uniqueness with me. Share your vibrancy, your quest, your wisdom. Share your deep and wide and open heart.

Tell me how you got to where you are from where you were. I, too, need guidance on the journey. Talk to me of courage and curiosity, of reconciliation and redemption. I want to know who you are. I want you to know me. For we are treasures, we mature women. We are repositories of wisdom and of strength.

Here are some of my stories, dear friend. Perhaps you'll puzzle out their meanings even as you share your own stories with me. Life stories. Life lessons. Life celebrations. This is how you live a life. We did it. You can too.

THREE QUESTIONS

> *My mind is changing dramatically as I move toward fifty. And I imagine fifty as some sort of a gate; the door is going to open and I'm going to be somebody else.*

PAULA GUNN ALLEN

Everyone has a story.

Tell me yours.

My original intention for this book was to go out with my trusty tape recorder and pad and pen and interview women from fifty to eighty, women who have been there, done that, and want to tell the world, "Here I am. This is my story." A good and grand plan and one I began with zest and hopefulness. But what I found! Ah, what I found!

What *did* I find? I found distilled wisdom in the midst of all too familiar tales of struggle, of love betrayed, of marriage and motherhood and losing and leaving and starting over. I found poverty and prejudice. I found yearning and bitterness, terror and triumph. No complacency. No rigidity. No ossified, unconscious, unaware lives. More courage than contempt, more desire than despair. In short, what I found were tales of acquired wisdom. What I found was gallantry.

The world has changed so much since the women I know were born. And no roles and expectations have changed as much as those of women who grew up during the First or Second World War, who moved from the waltz to the Charleston, from jitterbugging to square-dancing, from dancing with lovers to dancing alone.

So I began to ask my compatriots, both the generation that came before me and the generation I call my own, to answer three questions. I did want to hear their life stories, edited in memory, but the themes seemed the same. Only the details changed. I wanted to know what they knew. I wanted them to pass it on to other women, those in their generations and those in mine, and the women coming after, all those bright, energetic baby-boomers and Gen-Xers who might want some bread crumbs thrown along the path to lead them safely through the forest.

Here are the questions:

What are the three most important events in your life, and what have you learned from them?

What do you regret most, if anything, in your life?

What three things would you like to pass on to other women, from your wisdom and experience?

In fairy tales, it's always three, and only three. Three wishes. Three trials. Three temptations.

It's not what happens to you, but what you *do* with what happens to you. It's not what actually happens, but what you perceive as happening. It's not the event, but the meaning attached to the event.

And so the women I know shared the meanings in the

events attached to their lives. Some preferred to remain anonymous. Some preferred not to give their ages. Some were in the middle of whirlwinds and so could not yet assess the import of what they were going through. But they all had gifts to share. I call these gifts "acquired wisdom," and I will share all of them with you. They have helped me.

My friend Alicia told me that she regretted nothing in her life. "I'm not going to waste time thinking 'What if?' I did the best that I could, when I could, as I thought I should." My friend Mary echoed this thought. "I did my best when I knew enough to do so." A woman who had lost the use of her right leg and had to learn to handle the disfigurement told me that the most difficult thing for her was pride. "I let pride get in my way when I returned to work, when I needed help. The lesson I learned that I want to pass on to other women is that of taking one step at a time. Literally."

Several women reported that the most important event in their lives was the birth and the raising of their children. "I always hurried life," said one respondent, "waiting for my child to grow up, looking ahead to the end of my schooling so that I could support her better, looking ahead to some distant day in which all the waiting would be over, waiting for my life to take a different turn. It is only now that I realize what a gift my daughter was to me. I can never get back those years. Now, in my fifties, I have learned to live more day-to-day, cherishing each day, cherishing her."

Many women cited earlier mistaken marriages as important events that changed their lives. Mary Jane, a body/mind therapist who has remarried, listed walking away from a bad marriage as one important event, her schooling as a second, and remarrying a kind and compatible man who supports her quest for knowledge as the third. Her only regret? "I regret that I have used so much of my energy trying to make others happy and fixing things for them. It doesn't work."

One woman, who is the lay director of a Methodist church, told of her faith deepening as she grew older, and of feeling as if she walked hand in hand with her God. This spirit-strengthening was echoed by women who continued the difficult tasks of caregiving while struggling to find balance and meaning in their lives. My friend Mary gave her Rolex watch to her daughter, who had just graduated from pharmacy school. "I don't care about material things the way I did in my twenties and thirties and forties. I don't care about a new car or a luxury car. My study of Buddhist philosophy has helped me to become more peaceful in my life, living in the now, instead of regretting the past or struggling to discern the future."

The women who made their later lives ones of artistic freedom were especially emphatic about the new-found time and energy that they could devote to their craft, although some still struggled with concerns of love and duty and financial hardship. "I can finally put myself out there without reservation," said one artist. And another: "I pour myself onto every page. This is my life now. It's taken me half a lifetime to learn who I am, and what I can do. The rest of my lifetime I will do it."

Within the pages of this book, you will find stories of devotion and determination, of courage and caring, of family loyalties and solitary independence. I have divided the book into sections: "Mature Authenticity," "Body Blessed," "Emotions Passionate," "Mind Radiant," and "Spirit Strengthened"; but many of the stories flow into others. A woman's sexual life includes emotions. A story on families embraces emotional genealogy. A meditation on the body includes thoughts on the outer images we present to the world through decades of closet clothes. A caregiver's story is physical, emotional, and spiritual. Creativity and the mind includes the creativity of spirit and the passion of emotions. Laughter mixes with regret, and love lost with strength regained, and aging well becomes not only the best revenge but the only wise and joyful game in town.

There are many other stories in this book. From the woman who left her husband because of a chance comment that brought her face to face with herself, to an old woman dancing on a summer greensward at dawn. From the woman who climbs mountains to the women who take care of their dying loved ones. From the baked-potato lady to the woman who's still juicy, from the well-married woman to the woman who throws herself into her art with passion. There are good ol' girls, there are bag ladies and immigrant teachers. There's a woman who created "a chair for my lover" and a woman who was once "a million-dollar baby in a five-and-ten cent store." There are women still struggling with the unfinished business of the past, and women who soar creatively to the heights. There's advice for granddaughters and acts of gratitude. There are sisters and other strangers and women who dream the self into being day by day. There are women with too many teakettles alongside women with shabby underwear and all things unloving. A wealth of questions. A wealth of women. A wealth of answers.

I'll ask you those same three questions, dear reader. What are the three important events in your life, and what have you learned from them? What do you regret most, if anything, in your life? What three things would you like to pass on to other women, from your wisdom and experience? I've answered those questions for myself. Now it's your turn. All our answers are secret. All our answers are wise and true for each of us. It's a sacred task, isn't it, to sum up individual private joys and private despairs, distill the wisdom, and pass on the gifts of what we have learned to others? I'm learning still. From every woman I meet who tells her story. From every woman with three questions, three wishes, three trials, three temptations, three regrets, three resolutions. Acquired wisdom. Continuing wisdom. Shared wisdom. So I will ask you, through every story you read and resonate with in this book, to tell me your story. And I will tell you mine.

MATURE AUTHENTICITY

*When I look into the future, it's so bright it burns
my eyes.*

W hen I think of mature authenticity, I think of a painting
I once had on the wall of a home that burned down years ago.
The painting was of golden, endless wheat fields, fat, thick
strokes of shades of sun and late high summer that matched
the sun that shone on the figure of a woman, indistinct in age,
who stood in the middle of the golden grain, raising her arms
to the clear blue sky.

I am that woman. Perhaps you are too. After years of ex-
posure to the merciless elements, to the sway and the turning
of the seasons, we have come to the end of summer. We have
come to the time of harvest. We have come into our full matu-
rity. Like a cornucopia of harvest grains and vegetables, we
are full, bursting, overflowing with plenty onto the tables of
Thanksgiving.

In the Episcopal church I grew up in, there is a Thanksgiving hymn I used to sing.

> Come ye thankful people come.
> Raise the song of harvest home.

All is safely gathered in,
Ere the winter storms begin.

It expresses to me the full bounty of being the age that I am.

For many of us, that age of harvest begins as we turn fifty. For some of us, the sixties or even the seventies are the decades of fullness. Any or all of the above. There is no time limit on authenticity. To paraphrase an old prayer, "We have learned the things that we ought to have learned, we have done the work that we ought to have done, and yes—there is health and abundance in us."

Never mind the world recognizing the depth and the breadth of our talents, our experiences, our knowledge, and our mature hearts. The world, for the most part, is still engrossed in the flickering shadows of skinny, young, beautiful, impossibly groomed images that bear little relation to us. Never mind, we've got their number. We know the truth of who we are.

This book is a reminder of that truth. It is a celebration of the mature feminine. There are no tips on dieting in this book. There is no plan to snare a mate. There are no rules for getting ahead. There is no attempt to change your outer image, although there are no rules against it.

This is a book about essence, rather than appearance. This is a book about recognizing and rejoicing and embracing your life, at whatever age, at whatever crossroad, in whatever situation. This is a book about your own inner, feminine, divine wisdom and your own dynamic, energetic presence.

We are the best-kept secret in America. No moaning and groaning, no ranting and raving. The superficial cannot coexist with a wise and loving and mature heart. Waste no energy trying to change the world's perceptions. Change your own perceptions, and rejoice in who you are. You are a courageous, loving, powerful woman who has much to give the world. Rejoice and be thankful. Celebrate your harvest home.

Body Blessed

Health,
Healing,
Sex, and
Body
Image

BODY BLESSED

Your power in this life derives not from your ability to produce, but rather from your ability to balance the in-flow and out-flow of spirit. And at the root of this ability, your teacher, the breath, moves quietly in and out, automatically regulating and meeting your needs. Observe and listen to this teacher. It will lead you to great harmony.

ELLEN MEREDITH

I am taking a yoga class, designed especially for women and men who have either had injuries or surgery or who are over sixty. I love this class. The teacher, Lucy, who is slender, flexible, and young—but not too young—is quietly encouraging, with a depth of patience I have found only in first-grade teachers. She is as nourishing as the homemade bread that she sells in the foyer three times a week.

The class is called "Gentle Yoga" in the brochure, and so it is, for anyone who is in shape. I'm not. I used to practice yoga, but that was many years ago. Oh, what has happened to my Shoulder Stand? My Sun Salutation? At least I'm good with the Pranayama, the breathing techniques. But we are not supposed to compare ourselves with others. We are not supposed to compete, even with ourselves. We are to stretch but not struggle. An apt metaphor for awareness and acceptance. I am peaceful in this class. It is like coming home. I want no chatter, just a concentrated awareness of both my body's limitations and my body's strengths. I find this soon enough.

I am attempting to balance gracefully in Tree Pose, with one foot on the floor and one foot raised to my ankle, knee, or thigh, depending on flexibility, and my arms positioned gracefully above me, reaching for the sky like branches. But I am not graceful anymore. What I am is frustrated. I lose my balance again and again. My knees creak and my toes hurt. I set my mouth in a nonpeaceful line. I will make this happen for me.

Then I notice another woman next to me in the class. She is attempting the same pose. But she is doing it with thick woolen socks on her feet, in order to protect the foot that is partially amputated. Oh my God! She can manage, however clumsily, even with one foot half-gone and no way to balance evenly. I think of the old proverb—yes, I do!—the one about cursing the fact that you have no shoes until you meet someone who has no feet. I am humbled. I think of the woman I used to be, the slender, young, vibrant, flexible woman who ran races and shone brightly in her yoga class and elsewhere, with a boundless energy and enthusiasm that made no compromises for illness, who made no compromises for anything as devastating as amputated feet.

The woman I am watching is serene. For a moment she keeps her balance, then rests her feet, first the strong one, then the half-one, and smiles at me ruefully as if to say, "See! I'm doing the best I can, and that's enough."

Oh body blessed! When did I stray so far from honoring the body that I have now, the one that sags and bags and huffs and puffs, and tires easily while my mind is still exercising joyfully? When did I decide that my body had to look a certain way and perform a certain way, and never, never give in to the slings and arrows of outrageous fortune? When did I let other people's perceptions judge and denigrate my sturdy, faithful, less than perfect body?

I've never thought of my body as a technical marvel, as a machine. No, it's not an old car that will rust out or a computer that will crash. It is a container for spirit. A living, breathing, moving container that holds my mind, my emotions, my very soul.

Long ago I read of the fourfold person, who lives in a space bounded by the four pillars of life. This person incorporates into her being the mind, the emotions, the spirit, and the body, all continually fed, all continually balanced. The dance of life itself is the exquisite balancing of these four pillars. Within the realm of the body are all the externals by which we measure and judge our lives. So, too, do some of us measure and judge with the mind, measure and judge by the emotions. Only spirit, or so it seems to me, is constant and unchanging, ageless, creative, caring. Only spirit cannot be judged and found wanting.

In some spiritual traditions, the body is an intricate map. Within each body there are certain places—call them energy fields or call them spiritual centers—where the attributes and qualities of the Self reside. Not the little self, who is often selfish or self-absorbed or self-willed, but the radiant, unchanging Self, the pattern of the True Self. This Self is the Oversoul of the individual smaller, active, outer self, which includes, of course, the self that has to deal with the body and the mind and the emotions as they change, as they age. This is the Core Self, the Self that oversees the pattern of your life.

I remember this and more, as we sink onto our mats and prepare for meditation. The teacher's voice is soothing, the music barely heard above the whisper of my body, as it talks to me, protesting this muscle, settling down and lengthening here, giving a twinge of discomfort there. What started as frustration against the vicissitudes of the body has turned into an appreciation of its courage and its strength. What is left, both in this breathing room and in my body, is the in-flow and out-flow of spirit throughout my body temple.

Oh body blessed! How I have railed against you. How I have despaired of you. How I have allowed you to be despised and hated and feared and denigrated and judged by others and myself.

No more! You are strong and sturdy and functional. You have served me well. I can still call you beautiful within my heart and mind and within the pattern of my True Self. Oh body blessed! I find to my surprise and delight that I do love you after all. And I will cherish you.

NACHOS FOR BREAKFAST

> *We are indeed much more than we eat, but what we
> eat can nevertheless help us to be much more than what
> we are.*
>
> ADELE DAVIS

$\mathcal{O}$ne of my cousins just lost her husband to cancer after several anguished years. Three years ago, her father died as well. She and my other cousin rotated his care for several months in their respective homes. My cousin is tough, strong, caring, stubborn. She has five grown children who love her and a low-paying night job for which she is overqualified. She is sixty-two, with knee and back and eye problems. Determined to survive. Devastated by her losses. We talk on the phone from nearby towns.

"I can't get out of my nightgown," she tells me. "Except to go to work. I can't pay my bills. I can't clean my house. I can't do anything."

"What are you eating?" I ask her. I know her body is exhausted, her emotions are overwhelming, and her nerves are shot. "Ice cream," she tells me, trying to laugh through her tears. "That's all I want. No use cooking for one person. Ice cream for supper, go to work each night, potato chips and

Diet Cokes all the way home in the middle of the night, to this empty house. Sleep and get up and start again. Gallons of ice cream."

"Get dressed now," I order her. If we lived in the same town, I would go to her house and yank her out of it by the hair. "Go for a walk, go to the grocery store, go to a salad bar. For God's sake, take care of yourself."

She refuses. She has never taken advice from anyone in her life.

"What are you eating?" she asks me.

"A green salad, fresh zucchini and corn, and a dab of brown rice." I think of my careful, orderly mother, and wonder if in my old age I am becoming just like her.

"How boring," she says, echoing my own thoughts. "How can you cook for just one person?" she cries. "I'll never cook again."

"Okay by me," I say. "But please, please, please, at least open a can of soup. Please take care of yourself."

"You don't understand," she wails. But of course I do. We have both had huge losses over the last decade. After pleading with her to feed herself, I hang up and go to my now-cold supper.

I do understand. She knows I understand. Once I ate nothing but nachos for breakfast. I was in my late forties, had left my husband, and was going through a long, difficult, scary, poverty-stricken divorce. I lived in a semifurnished one-bedroom apartment, taught at the community college at night, and supplemented my income by selling what copies I could of my first self-help book and by lecturing at churches and community centers. The only way I could seem to keep hysteria at bay was to run for miles in the early morning (I was fit, svelte, and younger then), and after a long, hot shower where I let my troubles go down the drain, I would walk to a small neighborhood cafe, timing my arrival for its opening. Then I would eat nachos for breakfast. Almost every day.

Oh the bliss of it all! I would order the large, with refried beans, melted cheese, crisp fried tortilla chips, all layered with a sprinkling of jalapeño peppers on top. The first fiery bit of the jalapeños would bring tears to my eyes. I reasoned that the acrid, vinegary slices, with their searing aftermath, were, at the very least, good for my sinuses, and also could be counted as a green vegetable. The savage crunch into the salty chips alleviated my anger. I chomped my way through them. Ah, the first taste of the layers of oily, runny, melty cheese over the earthy warmth of the beans. How satisfying! How sustaining! How rebellious! Damn the cholesterol. Full speed ahead!

It took almost a year to obtain my freedom. And I mourned the eighteen previous years of marriage for many months more. Three years later, I mourned the death of my ex-husband as well, just one year after the loss of a beloved son. So I do understand ice cream for supper and nachos for breakfast. I understand how hard it is to feed yourself, to sustain yourself, to nourish yourself, to nurture yourself. I understand the fears in the middle of the night and the tears at dawn. But neither ice cream for supper nor nachos for breakfast will fill the empty places in your heart.

"One day at a time," my cousin says bravely through her tears, the next time we talk. A good truism to cling to. We arrange to meet for lunch at a soup-and-salad place. She's coming along. In a few more weeks—a few more months, tops—she'll discard the ice cream for supper and put her life in order. She'll learn how to nourish herself alone, like thousands of women before her. I'm optimistic about her future. After all, I got through, didn't I? At least I don't eat nachos for breakfast anymore.

THE SOUL OF WALKING

> *I will tell you what I have learned myself. For me, a long five- or six-mile walk helps. And one must go alone and every day.*
>
> BRENDA UELAND

$\mathcal{O}$ne of my dearest friends, Rita Robinson, wrote a book called *The Soul of Walking*. A tall, slender, vibrant redhead about my age, she strides around a five-mile lake in a ski resort town in California, with her huge Labrador retriever at her side. She does five miles around the lake most mornings, and neither rain nor sleet nor snow can keep her from her appointed rounds. I wish I had written the book she wrote. I'll borrow only the title, to illustrate my favorite way of being in the world. Walking. Walking with soul. Walking with joy. Walking with remembrance.

I am short and sturdy, with whitening hair, and no dog at my side, so I do not make the arresting picture—woman against the backdrop of mountains and lake—that my friend does. That's not the point, is it? I am one of an invisible army of foot soldiers, middle-aged and elderly, all shapes and sizes, who swing our arms and breathe deeply and put one foot in front of the other, and turn the daily maintenance of exercise into a quiet and private joy. When I don't have a chance to walk, I get cranky. And indoor mall-walking and indoor treadmills just aren't the same.

An aquaintance of mine from the Gentle Yoga class is a walker too. She hurt her hip and had to have surgery and the doctor told her, "Move your butt, woman!" and so she walks, whether her hip hurts or not, and the more she walks, the more it heals. I walk when my knees hurt and my back hurts too. It eases my joints. I see her most mornings, as we round the curves of the labyrinth of courts that form a perfect three miles and give each of us a view of the city as we get to the highest point in the road. There are two- and three-storey mansions on one side, throwbacks to an earlier, southern sensibility, and woodland, park, and zoo below. I know the zoo is there. I can hear the lions roaring in their cages far below. It never fails to pause me for a moment, remembering.

I am like so many women of my age. Memory laces itself through me, no matter what the season, no matter what the activity. I remember living on the other side of the park, a few miles away, in an old-fashioned house with a porte cochère where the carriages were meant to enter. I remember being in a Victorian marriage, where all the love and will in the world could not coax the marriage into even a semblance of joy. Both the marriage and the man are long gone. But where we were is always a part of where we are now. Memories can be healed, transformed, reduced to fact. But they cannot be erased.

It was only a dozen or so years ago that I walked through the large rooms of that house, room to room, pacing, caged, trapped, despairing, wondering if I could or would or should escape my fate. I could hear the lions roaring from the park when the wind blew a certain way.

The man I was married to and loved and left has been dead for ten years. Oh fellow women, do you know this story? Who has not been there, by the time we are fifty, or sixty, or seventy? Who has not left or been left? Whether by design, intention, or fate, we remain solitary, remembering.

Now, today, this instant, I walk briskly and joyfully in the open air, arms swinging, head uplifted to catch the breeze. Sunlight falls on my hair and eyelids. I should have worn a hat. I sweat and grunt a little, going uphill around the curve. The soles of my feet mark my passing. The soul of the solitary me takes note, rejoices. The lions roar in the park below me. They are caged. I am free. And so I go my way, rejoicing.

No Organ Recitals

When you can't remember why you're hurt, that's when you're healed. When you have to work real hard to re-create the pain, and you can't quite get there, that's when you're better.

Jane Fonda

$\mathcal{M}$y maternal grandmother, who taught me so much about being a woman, grew more outspoken as she grew older. One day she told me, after an exasperating and lengthy phone call from one of her friends, "No more organ recitals!"

"When you have something wrong with you, you can tell your story three times," she advised. "You can tell it to your doctor, you can tell it to your family, and you can tell it to one friend. But what I can't abide is someone who can't shut up about their insides and what's wrong with them."

I took her advice to heart. I suggest you do too. Oh, you may have to stretch the rule a little at times. When you are writing or painting or dancing, you need to revise and refine and update your story occasionally. But give your friends and relations and coworkers a break, and don't expound on the intimacies of your personal body temple. I believe whole-heartedly in doing the work of the body and the work of the emotions and the work of the mind and the work of the soul. I just don't tell everyone in town.

But some women I know use illness as their personal metaphor for life. It's what sets them apart. It's what makes them different. It's who they are. Harsh words, harsher than those my grandmother used.

I don't mean to be unkind. I certainly have alluded, more than once, both privately and in my work, to illness and to the continuing fear of debility that it has awakened in my psyche. But unless you're writing a book about healing, spare me the details.

You are more than your aches and pains. You are more than what you have suffered, are suffering, or expect to suffer. The body has powerful messages that force us to pay attention. It's happened to me. But I am more than those messages, and I don't need to broadcast them to the world.

When I was growing up, a lady did not reveal, to all and sundry, the details of her bowels or the removal of her womb. Now we are forced to endure blow-by-blow accounts of everything that is being removed or has passed its prime. I think it's good sense and refreshing and high time that we women, especially older women, know how our bodies work in every detail and thus take charge of our bodies and what we want to do with our private parts. But you don't have to make a career out of your organ recitals.

A counselor once told me that people *do* need to repeat their stories, until they come to an understanding of what that story means, until they come to forgiveness, until they come to resolution. But she, too, had a rule.

"You can tell your story three times to me," she told a group who had gathered to explore solutions to healing.

"Then you need to get past the broken record, and be silent, and reflect, and look at the story from every angle of vision you possess, and learn, and then give it up. Don't keep ripping the bandaid off to see if the hurt has healed."

This is more serious than my grandmother's exasperation with organ recitals, but it is similar. Similar enough for me to hope that when you tell your friends (and you will) about your latest difficulty, whether illness or adversity, you will also, at some point, be still. Be silent. Work it through. Spare others, even as you nurture yourself. And please, no more organ recitals.

EASY BEING GREEN

> *Once we recognize what it is we are feeling, once we recognize we can feel deeply, love deeply, can feel joy, we will demand that all parts of our lives produce that kind of joy.*

AUDRE LORDE

*D*ebby Roth is an old friend of mine who wrote a beautiful, life-affirming book called *Being Human in the Face of Death.* Although she designed the book to help professional and family caregivers deal with terminal illness, in the midst of writing she was diagnosed with breast cancer herself. So she included a wry essay on how it felt to be on the other side of the caregiver equation, to be the patient instead of counseling the client, as she had done in her work at the Center for Help in Time of Loss.

One of the things she talked about was the urgency she felt to change her immediate surroundings, once she had returned home from the hospital and taken up residence again in her Manhattan apartment. "I was obsessed by rearranging furniture and adding plants and light to my room. I even went in search of an indoor fountain so that I could have the sense of being near water in a city apartment. Each new thing I added to the decor seemed to require a shift in the balance. A new ashtray made a lamp look out of place, a new pillow changed the color flow. What seemed like a simple diversion into decorating gave me a new perspective on this human experience. . . . I felt in the deepest core of myself an urge toward integrity. I felt there was a rightness to all things, based on balance and wholeness. . . ."

Another friend of mine hates the winters in Texas. She is a prime example of SAD (Seasonal Affective Disorder) throughout the damp, cold months, which to someone living in the north or midwest would seem to be relatively light, mild winters. She fills her house with green plants and adds color everywhere, to take the chill off of sleety, gray days. She comes alive in the hot, lush, baking heat of summer, while others around her droop in the heat.

Of course there is a correlation between sunshine and health, light and health, color and health, green things growing and health. But another friend of mine took the color issue a quantum leap forward. When her small company was embroiled in a complicated contract dispute with two much larger companies, who stonewalled her and passed the buck at every turn, she felt blocked, depressed, and powerless. After weeks of struggle, she was advised by a colleague to surround herself with green. "Think green, pray green, meditate green. They owe you money. You've exhausted outer avenues. You have to work with the inner realm. Think green."

My friend went out and bought herself a set of green sheets, which she slept on every night. And of course she thought, affirmed, meditated, prayed, and worked to resolve

44

the situation amicably, without resorting to a lawsuit. After three days of concentrating on green and laying herself down to sleep on sheets the color of money, the situation was resolved and she received her money. Coincidence? Magic? I couldn't say.

"It's not easy being green," Kermit the Frog tells us on *Sesame Street*. Of course he's talking about being different from the others around him. You're different too. Wiser, hopeful, gutsy, valuable, irreplaceable. So it *is* easy being green. It doesn't take a great stretch of the imagination or a large outlay of time or money. Think green. Whether you're regaining your own inner harmony after major surgery, or sniffling and down and out after a long, cold, dreary winter, or fighting for your money and your rights as a businesswoman, think green. Think joy, harmony, balance, wholeness. Think empowerment. Think new life and new seasons and new wealth. And if all else fails, sleep on green sheets and ask for dreams of color and light. And let the green light beam you forward when it comes.

BAKED-POTATO LADY

> *"Large middle-aged ladies should never wear brown,"*
> *my mother stated categorically. "It makes them look*
> *like a baked potato." She paused and delivered. "As*
> *they get older, a wrinkled baked potato."*

FROM *LEARNING L.A.*

*T*he above excerpt is the beginning of a comic novel I wrote called *Learning L.A.,* about a middle-aged rural woman who sets off on a Wizard of Oz odyssey from Texas to California. But the words themselves came from my own mother, who had so many rules and regulations about what a woman—beg pardon, a lady!—should wear. She got these rules from her own southern mother and grandmother, who gave out advice more freely than cookies.

I learned a lot of useful things from my mother and my grandmother. They are my strength. Manners and thoughtfulness, civility and kindness, and a host of other qualities that made them the women that they were. l learned a lot of useless things as well, trivial notions that haunt me to this day and serve no purpose. The process of sifting out the gold from the dust is for me, for most of us, a lifelong task.

The thread of this essay is a doubled one, two single

threads twisted together, two stories meant for a single destination.

But which destination? I have not finished the novel because my heroine cannot decide whether to go home again, or whether she can ever get back from who she is to who she once was. I don't know the answer.

I was taught that gloves should be worn in church and hats should be worn to funerals and of course, as every woman knows, white shoes must never appear after Labor Day. And if you are a large, middle-aged lady, you never wear brown, for fear of being mistaken for a baked potato.

When I came home again, after a seven-year odyssey in L.A., I didn't fit. I had outgrown my past and my mother's rules. I had traveled the world and been changed at depth. I cared little for what the world (and my mother) thought, but I didn't want to hurt anyone's feelings. I was a twisted double thread that kept unraveling. I was also a grown woman shaped by adult adversity as much as by a golden childhood.

How do you sort it all out? How do you keep the eternal verities you have learned in culture and tribe, values that have stood you in good stead while exploring other lands and other peoples? Yet, now larger and wiser than when you left, how do you blend the old and the new, the hard-won with the home-grown? Individuation continues at any age.

I have kept the kindness and discarded the rules. I have kept the love and discarded the trivial. But I have yet to buy and wear a brown dress, although earth tones suit both my coloring and my disposition.

Will total freedom come for me when I can march into a

store and buy a shapely, A-line, warm and earthy dress that becomes me? Is it too late for an image makeover? Could there be shoes to match, but never hat and gloves? Liberation advances in small steps. Because, after all is said and done, no one wants to look like a baked-potato woman.

MEMORY CLOTHES

The Dust Bowl overlaid on the Great Depression taught us to "use it up, wear it out, make it do, or do without."

MARY TULLIS KUNDE

$\mathcal{I}$ have a lot of stuck-in-closet clothes. Clothes that never see the light of day or rest upon my body. These are not clothes that I rummage through daily, looking for something comfortable, large, loose, and practical to wear. For I can't abide anymore tight, rigid, constructed costumes.

Working out of my home, I need clothes that flow, that move, that breathe. Cotton casuals all. But what to do, what to do, what to do, when I am called upon to travel, to lecture, to go to a professional function? The power suits, the investment dressing that was extolled in the '80s—ah what a decade made up of image!—stand rigidly at attention in my closet still. I refuse to buy more. So even if most of them are too small, a few too big, and hardly any just right, I keep them for that day when I will be required to costume myself again and sally forth to show the world who I am by the clothes I wear.

I open the door and sigh deeply. What can I keep, what can I wear, what can I give away? In this corner are certain items I refuse to part with. The robe belonging to my son Michael that I clutched to me after he died, that still carries his essence; a skirt made out of ribbons my grandmother made me twenty years ago; a jacket that belonged to the only lover I had after my divorce. Even my favorite suit, the one I wore to another son's wedding. I gave away the funeral clothes though. I wear them only once and discard them. I've gotten rid of a lot of dresses that way. But these clothes are full of memories. How can I let them go?

Oh, I do give away a lot of my clothes. I give away most anything I haven't worn in a year or two, just like the magazine articles say. I give away to my friends and family and the women's shelter. But I keep my costume clothes (they are far too expensive to replace at this time in my life) and I keep my memory clothes.

My clothes are my history. My follies and my fortunes stare at me mutely whenever I open the closet door.

I follow all the rules about clothing that I gleaned over the years. Ideas about color and texture, the way you're supposed to separate your clothes into categories and hang ribbons or colored curtain dividers between, so that you will not, by some mistake, wear clothes to one function that are meant for another. Sort of like the seven-days-a-week panties my mother used to buy me as a teenager. God forbid if we ever wore Tuesday's panties on Thursday, or vice versa! We actually had the days of the week embroidered on our fannies.

Here are clothes I bought or borrowed or were given to me when I tried out new personalities. I know too well who I am now. Here is my life in my closet. I can trace it, from fondly remembered scarves that never wear out, to shoes (no more high heels ever again!), to purses (does anyone ever really need more than three or four purses at the most?). In color, in fabric, in cut and style, in expanding and shrinking, in riches and in poverty, in sickness and in health, these are my clothes. Here is my life. Here am I.

So I go in and sort them out again, year by year, memory by memory. Then I give everything I can bear to part with away. Again. For every ten items I give away, I can buy one new thing, I calculate, a thrifty old trick taught to me by my daughter-in-law. I seldom buy new clothes, however.

Sometimes the clothes refuse to go. Instead, they seem to multiply, like coat hangers do, except that these coat hangers are filled. Filled with a changeable life and a changeable body, my life stares back at me on hangers. What, oh what, shall I do? Shall I take them all out and give them all away and start over from scratch, naked and new, a blank canvas full of possibilities? Or shall I lean toward thriftiness, alter what I can, make odd combinations of lonely sweaters and blouses that have no matching pants? Shall I go for the minimalist look, all white T-shirts and blue jeans, one coat, a pair of jogging shoes? What's a body to do?

I calculate. I've bought fewer than ten new items of clothing in the past three years, not counting underwear, socks, and some hideous corrective shoes prescribed when I sprained my foot. Surely that's a record for an American twentieth-century woman? But other priorities predominate. I'm simply not a consumer anymore.

I close the closet door gently. Another day. Stay for now.

I wonder *why* they do it. It takes so much time, effort, denial, projection of image outward, masks in place. Objects of beauty, they exist for approval.

Maybe it's sour grapes. Maybe I need to put more effort into the outer. But I am comfortable inside my skin.

"No shoes. Leotards optional. Makeup is not required." So says my movement teacher, the woman who has worked with me for over a year to strengthen my back and my right foot after injuries. I think I'll take that for my motto.

However do we women of a certain age find the balance between a healthy consideration of the body's needs, appropriate covering for the self-same, much-used body, and appropriate grooming to go out into the world and interact with others, according to our life's external requirements? No shoes are required for my work, only when I sally forth outside. No leotards or other costumes are required for my exercising hours. Just sweats and, yes, good shoes when I walk. No makeup, I have come to discover, is ever required of me. I seldom wear it anymore, only when some sort of a sop to convention is needed. It seems more of a mask than ever. My face is more naked now. It suits me better.

What if we mature women staged a revolution? What if we wore just what we wanted to wear, for ease and comfort? What if shoes were seldom required, leotards or power suits never, and all the drawers and dressing tables and shoeboxes full of old makeup were put in a landfill, for anthropologists to discover a hundred years from now? We'd have a lot of toxic waste to explain. The beauty and fashion industry would fold, as would the magazines and diet books that support it. Oh, we would still put cream on our faces and lotion on our hands and soap on our bodies. Maybe a little lip gloss. Maybe highlights here and there. But the slaves would revolt, the slaves would be free.

How individual we would all be, striding through our neighborhoods with old clothes on and bare faces. How un-fettered, self-accepting, free! What would people think? How could we define ourselves? Certainly not by status, cost, class, shape, or size. How would we be known then? How would we be recognized? praised? noticed? approved of? lusted after? admired? promoted? loved?

You tell me.

SAFE SEX REVISITED

*I doubt that I shall have affairs or bother my children
when they are grown, for my real passion always goes to
writing.*

MICHELE MURRAY

*M*y youngest son, Robert, who works in publishing, called
me with excitement in his voice. "Mom," he said, "did you
know that you are in a book called *Spiritual Literacy?* They've
reprinted one of your *Soulwork* essays. It's in the section on
spiritual literacy and the body."

"Which essay?" I asked, envisioning some soulful and
heartful account of my spiritual journey. "It's called 'Safe
Sex,'" he said. I groaned. "Not *that* one. I can't believe I ever
revealed myself enough to write about my solution to both
celibacy and the AIDS crisis."

Well, I did. And it was published. And people read it. Here
is a piece of it again.

*Walking is safe sex for me. You see, you take your deep, sigh-
ing breaths and your hair tosses in the wind and you lift your
chin a little to gulp in more fresh air, and you close your eyes a
little against the warmth of the emerging sun, and your feet and*

your legs pump in unison and your thighs rub against each other in a rhythm, and you perspire a lot, and your T-shirt and shorts fill with moisture until you could wring them out by the time you've done a mile or so, and you're panting during the second mile, and your joints are growing looser and warmer, and your mind is floating and swaying with the tops of the trees, and everything is, for a few blessed moments, right. Walking as orgasm.

And so I go my way, rejoicing.

"Mom," Robert said, "it's wonderful. You told the truth. You revealed yourself. Isn't that better than feeling the shadow of your mother peering over your shoulder as you write?"

Yes, it is. And the shadows of other ancestors as well, those proper southern women who didn't even know the names of certain parts of their anatomies, and certainly never articulated them to outsiders, much less in print. I remember one relative referring discreetly to an operation she had to have as "something to do with my private parts." Oh me! Will I ever escape my foremothers? Mostly, to get around this dilemma, I write about the soul.

"Work with passion" is one aphorism on my computer. I have worked with passion for many years. Between taking care of an elderly, ill mother for six years and writing for a living, is it any wonder that sex, safe or otherwise, has taken a back seat to the passions of the mind?

I remember a meditation group I was in years ago in L.A. We were working with PsychoSynthesis, a brilliant melding of the psychological and the spiritual, created by the late Roberto Assagioli. One of the meditations had to do with learning detachment. You were to say and to experience, "I have a body, but I am not my body. I have a mind, but I am not my mind. I have emotions, but I am not my emotions."

At the time, my emotions threatened to swamp me and pull me into a great undertow. I was recovering from a great grief and a lingering illness, so I gratefully welcomed anything that could help me to detach myself from the pain.

A woman in the group fascinated me. She was in her seventies, with a deep, cavernous face and a long, angular body, and she wore a flowing blue skirt and blouse that matched the intensity of her eyes. She was a poet, and had recently moved from another part of the country to live with her daughter and son-in-law. In a discussion she said, "Of course, I'm still looking for a mate. Hope springs eternal. Meanwhile, I'm writing my poems. I'll always have my poems. But I miss sex. I miss intimacy." I was struck, even then, by the matter-of-fact way she equated her gift of words with her (to my younger mind, incomprehensible) longing to be united again in a sexual relationship. How could anyone, I thought to my-self somewhat judgmentally, still be looking for sex, looking for intimacy, looking for a man (or a woman, for that matter) when she was in her seventies, by God!

"Just work with passion," I told myself, as I turned fifty, "just work with passion and everything will come out all right." I have a body, but I am not my body.

Two of my women friends, both divorced, on opposite sides of the country, have found love and sex and intimacy in their late fifties and early sixties. How have they done this? I have no idea. But I rejoice for them even as I wish my seventy-something woman from the meditation class her heart's desire.

Work with passion. Walk with passion. It can be done alone or in tandem. Reveal yourself, at whatever age, as a woman of passion. Embrace celibacy or keep on hoping, keep on looking, keep on wanting. Keep yourself ready. Take five-mile walks and five-minute cold showers or lie entwined with an elderly lover, on twisted, sweating, sun-drenched sheets. No wrong, no right way here. I wish you well.

But live with passion, no matter what you do.

I'm Still Juicy

I was what's called, rather unhandsomely, "highly sexed." But it was such a surprise that one could attract. It was like a stream finding out that it could move a rock. The pleasure of one's effect on other people still exists in age—what's called making a hit. But the hit is much rarer and made of different stuff.

ENID BAGNOLD

My friend Sara is tall, thin, rangy, with no hips and no bustline, frizzy red hair, and lots of interesting and well-lived wrinkles. She's also sixty years old and involved in a passionate, ongoing relationship with a man she has known for years. When I visit her in her cabin in the mountains of northern California, I see how she fills the space around her with health and vibrancy. This woman is alive! She is creatively self-employed, which means lots of nail-biting and wondering when the next check will come. She struggles with money issues even as she asserts a fierce independence that does not readily accept help from others. But Sara has one thing that many of my friends do not. She's got a great sex life! Most of us would trade a lot in order to be in her shoes.

"How do you do it?" I ask her. "Ever since I've known

you, ten years or more, you've been involved with someone. You used to tell me how the kitchen table rocked whenever you started a new relationship. You used to tell me how when you went out walking every day, even in the dead of winter, that you'd meet men and they would be so interested that they'd try to follow you home."

"Well," she tells me, "there was that two-year period, after my rocky affair with the mysterious Indian man, that I swore off men forever."

"He wasn't mysterious," I remind her. "He was just sullen. I'm glad that's over."

"Me too," she concurs. "But just because there's one sour apple in the barrel, doesn't mean I'm giving up apples."

"What words of wisdom do you have for the rest of us?" I ask her. "It's been a long time for me between hellos."

"Well, it obviously isn't my looks," she reflects. (Although I think that she is beautiful, she does not. This happens a lot with my friends of a certain age.) "And I live in an isolated setting, and I work alone, and I seldom travel, and I don't have any money, and I don't move in social circles. So I guess the only thing is that I *like* men. I like sex. I like to move in my body. And most of all . . ." she smiles at me mischievously. "I'm still juicy."

Emotions Passionate

Family,

Friends,

and

Passionate

Decisions

EMOTIONS PASSIONATE

*There is a vitality, a life force, an energy, a quickening,
that is translated through you into action, and because
there is only one of you in all time, this expression is
unique. And if you block it, it will never exist through
any other medium and will be lost.*

MARTHA GRAHAM

I want to be all used up when I die. To live a life so full, so
rich, so deep, so high, that I miss nothing. This intention
leads, alas and inevitably, to passionate emotions.

I remember one perfect evening just before Christmas, a
few years ago when I lived in L.A. My youngest son and I
were driving to Palm Desert, about three and a half hours
from the city, in order to join my older son's family for a traditional Christmas. Picture this if you will. A white convert-
ible, a youngish man with blond hair and freckles and glasses,
a plump, mature woman with glasses and silvery-gold hair,
the wind whooshing our hair about as we sailed along the
highway, singing songs in tune with the CDs on the car stereo.

My son happened to know Lucinda Williams, a country-
western singer from Austin, Texas, where he had lived previ-
ously, so we sang her songs along with her as we drove. One

song in particular moved us both to laughter and to joy. It was about wanting nothing more in life than an old house, music, friends, travel, and passion.

"Passion and kisses," I sang along with the music. "That's all I want, passion and kisses."

"No, Mom," said my son, laughing. "It's not passion and kisses. It's 'Passionate Kisses.' That's the name of the song."

"Oh," I said. "Well, I want more than passionate kisses. I want passionate emotions."

"Was there ever any doubt of that?" my son yelled back at me over the music. And we both laughed and sang as the smog and the lights of the city fell away and the darkness of the desert rose up all around us, until a huge, almost red full moon rose between the mountains to guide us on our way.

A sense of joy rose up from deep within me. "Remember this moment," I thought to myself. "It will never pass this way again." And I sought to freeze the moment in time—the sense of camaraderie, the going toward family warmth and rituals, the night and the music and the full moon rising. Oh how can it ever be recaptured? Even in remembering? It can't. Of course it can't.

But it existed, that full-out, flat-out, rising joy, as we sped away from all that held us in that complicated city that took so much and gave so much to me as I worked in the AIDS crisis and published books on death and dying and grief recovery. As we sped away to a Christmas where even though there were empty places at the table, people we loved who would never be with us at Christmas again, so too were there new memories, of four generations together again and again.

I used to think that I would drown in my emotions. Now I know better. I ride the rollercoaster of their ups and downs, their highs and lows. There are no bland years. There are no years of dullness. I can learn to ride the waves of my emotions now, to meet them and to feel them fully and to distill them and to use them.

All is not lost in pain. There's joy too. There's a passion for life as well, living so. With or without kisses along the way, in such a well-lived, well-experienced, emotionally passionate life.

EMOTIONAL GENEALOGY

What you do today influences your matrilineal lines in the future. The daughters of your daughters are likely to remember you, and most importantly, follow in your tracks.

CLARISSA PINKOLA ESTÉS

From my paternal grandmother I inherited a country woman's build, a porcelain skin that did not wrinkle until she was seventy, and a good appetite. From my father I inherited a cleft in the chin, long thin fingers, an abstracted introspection, a keen love of books, and a desire to be a writer. From my maternal grandmother I inherited no-nonsense stoicism, gentility, invincibility in the face of catastrophe (she was a widow in her forties, as was my own mother in her thirties), and the serene way she supported and fed a household of ten females during World War II. The genuine and boundless love she gave me, her capacity for hard work, her fortitude and her frugality, all were gifts from her to me. From my mother I inherited love of family and tradition (although I have rebelled much!), an analytical mind, the warmth and kindness she showed to all those around her, and a sense of duty, devotion, and devoutness.

I inherited, as well, lost hopes, dashed dreams, a tendency to want to please others at whatever cost to myself, repressed emotions (until I learned better), sentimentality, a tendency to worry coupled with a tendency to self-pity (which I fight at all costs!)—and an unreasoning optimism that only increases as I grow older.

In short, I am made up of all my ancestors, paternal, maternal, long dead and gone and some I never even knew, the dreamers and the doers, the movers and the shakers, the middle-class genteel teachers and frontier lawyers and the hardscrabble Depression-era country folk. A certain tilt of head, a hand gesture, the lift of an eyebrow—all evoke the shadows of those who have gone before me. Coded in my DNA, generation upon generation, are physical characteristics, mental acuity, emotional idiosyncrasies, and spiritual questionings.

As I grow older and hopefully wiser, I become more and more aware of those ancestral connections. They are strongest in the maternal line, because the women who have made me have shaped me as well. We are not only connected through the umbilical cord of grandmothers to mothers to daughters, but we are connected, as well, through those invisible threads that link us, one to the other, through generations upon generations.

It is no wonder that many elderly southern women become obsessed with genealogy. It is their narrative time-and-place line to the past.

What of emotional genealogy? They are those threads that offer continuity as we sort out, in our mature years, which

weeds to pluck out of our emotional gardens and which flowers to water and shine upon. It is a task I ponder often.

My mother is the woman I love most and am least like. My
maternal grandmother is the woman I identify with most. I
never knew my grandfathers, and my daddy—for whom I am
a dead ringer physically and mentally—died when I was nine-
teen.

I have traveled the world over, taken chances my mother was afraid of taking, created the books that my father
only dreamed of writing. Like my grandmother, I have supported many others besides myself. I gave birth to four fine
sons. Three of them live on. My four grandchildren shine in
the sun.

When I take down from the cupboard the flowered lilac
plate that belonged to my grandmother; when I eat my supper
on the table that was once hers, and then my mother's, and
now mine; when I pick wild roses and honeysuckle from the
branches outside my office and arrange them lovingly in the
cut-glass vase that once stood on my grandmother's side-
board; when I sleep in my grandmother's real brass bed, one
brought across the prairies from Tennessee to Texas after the
Civil War by *her* grandmother, then am I rooted and grounded
in safety. I am linked by lineage.

I, so individual, so passionately independent, so self-suffi-
cient, cannot escape my past. I no longer want to. I gather up
the threads of my forefathers and foremothers and lay them
all around me like the handmade afghan my grandmother
made me, the one I clutch around me for comfort in the dark.

HOW POSITIVE DO WE HAVE TO BE?

Without question, the number-one priority for midlife and older women right now is economic security. The poverty rate for women is about 65 percent higher for older women than for older men. . . . 25 percent of all women working now can expect to be poor in their old age.

MARY ROSE OAKAR, CONGRESSWOMAN

There's a wonderful book out now whose title asks, "How good do we have to be?" Its premise is one of forgiveness and being okay with ourselves. The "good enough" factor.

Lately I have been bombarded with messages, both from the books I evaluate and from people in passing, about the value of positive thinking. On the record, I will say that I value positive thinking, which beats negative thinking any day of the week, and have braced myself both for change and in the midst of difficulties by practicing the art of looking for the good in every situation, even when it seemed that there was no good to be had, nor rhyme nor reason either. But I recognize the negative as well. Denial of what is does not work well for me.

When I began writing this book, I wanted it to be a celebration of the seasons of a woman's life, a shout of gladness to the universe, a recognition of a woman's authentic self. We have done it all, and we have come through. I still want that.

But recently my best friend, a valued critic and even more valued cheerleader, said to me (and very kindly too), "Oh, I hope this book is going to be different. You've written so much about AIDS, death and dying, grief recovery, caregiving, and the deep recesses of the soul. Make this book happier. Make it lighter. Make it more perky."

I am not a perky person. What I consider mellow may be called melancholy by others. But her comments set me to thinking what I could say and what I could not, about the seasons, especially the later ones, of a woman's life. I decided then and there that it was impossible to write a book that stressed the positive and only the positive. For one thing, conflict is an essential part of story. And we all have stories to tell about our individual lives in all their diversity and richness, and how we came through.

How positive do we have to be? Well, as a fellow traveler, I can tell you that as an aging woman in today's Western culture, you will be faced with age discrimination and gender discrimination and image discrimination. You will probably, unless you are well-married for a lifetime, and well taken care of throughout and beyond your husband's life, be faced with poverty, whether or not you have or have had a business, a profession, an education. If you are a middle-aged, divorced, displaced homemaker, it is almost a certainty. You will probably, if you are a daughter, and especially if you are the oldest daughter and single, become the primary caregiver for your parents and assorted relatives. Even the luckiest of women will probably become the caregiver for her husband, and live an average of eighteen years after he is gone. Those of us who become the caregiver for a dying son or daughter have even more challenges to face. And even more grief. You will probably live alone for a good part of your life, and you will probably be celibate for a good part of that life, and you may very well have health problems as you age, and there may or may not be someone who loves you and who will help take care of you. You will need to earn a living far beyond normal retirement age, and you'd better be resourceful and frugal and— yes—optimistic, or else you'll never make it.

But you *will* make it. You will make it through aging, and illness, and caregiving, and loss, and death and dying, and all the various stages of life that we go through—we *all* go through—as part of living a long and fruitful and valuable life. You will learn from each challenge, each loss, each opportunity for change, each decade. But you will not be diminished. What you go through will make you wiser. Will help you to flower with compassion. Will teach you resilience. Will help you make a difference in the world. Will help you to live a full, whole life, shadow and sun, joy and sorrow, love and loss, all, all, all, and everything.

How good do you have to be for such a life? Just as good as you are right now, today. Measure your lifetime progress decade by decade, but do not judge. You are good enough. How positive do you have to be? Enough to keep on living, keep on growing, keep on learning. But not so much that you

77

deny, repress, smother, and negate the awful and the real that comes to you along the way. You are all that you have experienced. What does not kill you illuminates you.

There's room for joy too, in such a life. But if I were you, I'd give up perky. Doesn't work much past the teen years. Be wisdom's woman. Choose grace as well. You deserve it, in such a long-lived, well-lived, well-loved, and mellow life.

P O S S E S S I O N S

*In a single moment of our living there is our ancestral
and personal history, our future, even our death,
planted in us and already growing toward fulfillment.*

LINDA HOGAN

*S*pring cleaning time. Help me, someone! Tell me what to
sort and what to clean and what to give away and what to
throw away. Tell me what to keep that is of value to me, that
marks a passage in my life, that speaks to me of memory. Tell
me what to do with my mother's possessions, the ones she divided so carefully and precisely among her three daughters
and their children, and the ones I keep for her, her link to a
lifetime now changed so utterly, and yet she says to me still
that she might need her things, and so I keep them just for
her. Possessions that clutter and cover a whole room plus
closets, and spill over into all my other rooms as well. Cherished possessions, that came from *her* mother and her
mother's mother before that. Too many possessions with too
much meaning. I am enmeshed in my mother's life.

It took a solid week of ten-hour days, several years ago,
to help my mother, shaking with Parkinson's disease, to catalog and gift her possessions before she moved, taking some

of her things with her, to an assisted-living facility. Five years earlier, I had helped her move into the condo she loved so much and was now vacating, helped her move from an old house filled tidily and neatly, but filled, filled, filled, with possessions.

My two sisters and I, and our children and grandchildren, did not fight over any of my mother's possessions. Not when we moved her first, not when we moved her later, not when we moved her from one level of care to another, from one room to another, from one nursing home to another and yet another. We cherished her. We cherished the things she gave us. We shared with one another.

We gave away furniture, clothes, linens, dishes. To friends, to helpers, to church, to community shelters. We gave and we gave and we gave. Until my mother's life was encapsulated in one-half of a pleasant room in the best private nursing facility available, and reduced to one closet, one bookcase, three drawers, one nightstand, one phone, one TV, one wheelchair, and some family photographs and handmade quilts and pillows. From the time that one of my sisters and I first moved her from her home to the condo, in the summer of 1989, to this last living move, in 1997, we moved her eight times.

Remember the words to "September Song"? The song in which "the days dwindle down to a precious few"? So too do possessions. At least so it was for my mother. I keep my mother's clothes in my spare bedroom, and take them to her a few at a time. The only new things she really needs are socks, gowns, and sweaters. My sister and I give her all we can. We have done so for a very long time.

"Don't be melancholy," advises my best friend. "You've done the best you can for your mother. You're still doing the best you can. Just keep sorting."

My best friend lives in a large, two-storey house in the country, with her own possessions and those of her late husband, her mother, and her mother-in-law. She runs her own business and manages several other family properties. She's still sorting and rearranging and blending and redoing and bringing into harmony a wealth of family possessions.

I am a woman who has often walked away from houses and possessions. Twice I have been burned to the ground with no insurance and little money. Twice I have gone from one country to another and back again with only the clothes on my back and my children with me. Twice I have left long, difficult, irreconcilable marriages. Again and again I have started over. A new leaf. A clean slate. Good riddance. Ashes to ashes. And each time possessions fly to me and stick to me and fill up the spaces in my life.

I cherish my mother's possessions. I welcome the treasured antiques passed down from great-grandmother to grandmother to mother to me. These possessions evoke the very essence of those I have known and loved and are no more with me. So here's the conundrum. What to keep, what to love, what to cherish, what to honor? And what to share with others or consign to scrap heap? What is precious? What is detritus? Who owns what? What owns me?

I am more than caretaker, more than repository. What starts as an exercise in cleaning closets has taken me on a journey through my lifetime and the lifetimes of those I loved.

How to live among the dead and still create space within me and around me, for all the new, the creative, the singular, the true of me that longs to be expressed?

Where do I leave off and family possessions begin? I'm still sorting.

Writing Letters to Dead People

> *Depression is not an easy companion on your journey, but let her go with us for a while. In her bundle she carries the anger you have carefully frozen with frigid blasts of fear and kept nourished with your pain. Dare to accept the bundle, to accept your own wholeness. Dare to forgive what hurt you and stop reliving the pain. Dare to thaw your rage.*
>
> Grandmother Growth
> (Susun S. Weed)

A friend of mine who has been through major challenges and who has done diligent inner work along the way called me excitedly one morning. "I've discovered a freeing exercise," she told me. "It's writing letters to dead people."

She had done journaling and visualization and lots of other mind/body techniques along the way. But until now, she had not been able to free herself from painful and arbitrary and senseless acts of cruelty she had experienced as a child and young adult.

It's fine to say "Don't be a victim" in your life, but when difficulties occur before you are equipped to deal with them, it's all just words. So my friend, on the advice of her pastoral counselor, was told to write a letter a day for seven days to the person or persons she felt had wronged her. No holds barred. No need for grammar, punctuation, long sentences, or coherency. No one looking over her shoulder. No one telling her that gritted teeth and explosive anger and childlike despair are unbecoming to a lady.

"So I wrote and I wrote and I wrote," she told me. "And when I finished writing, I put the letter away for a day and then I added more the next day and the next, until what took hours of privacy finally petered out to numbness and relief. I wrote it all. And then the letters began to change. There was more softness, more understanding, after all the hurt. I just couldn't keep the rage going. It had spent itself on paper. Then I did a little ceremony. I took a stainless steel bowl and I tore up the pieces of the letters, bit by bit, and I lit a match and burned it all. I sent the smoke up to the sky. I said the word 'release' again and again. I took the charred remains and sprinkled water on them. I scattered the dried remains. And now I feel so light and free. Isn't that amazing? The energy just pours out of me and onto the page and then is transformed by the telling and by the burning and by the releasing.

"And then, I forgave him," she said simply. "How could I not? And it was worth it. Whether it took seven days or seven nights or seventy times seven. By the act of writing and releasing, I forgave him."

"What's next?" I asked her.

"More letters to dead people," she said. "But not all at

once. I need to feel this freedom first. Then I'll concentrate on others. Maybe I'll write letters to live people too. Not to hurt them. Not to send. Just to free myself. Just to heal."

"What will you say?" I asked her.

"I don't know. I'll let the act of writing tell me."

"And then you will be free."

"*Then* I will forgive. And *then* I will be free," she corrected me.

"Amen," I said to her. And went to find a yellow pad and my favorite pen. To write a letter. To let the words pour down in tracks of emotion. I know just the bowl to use to tear the strips into. I know just the words to say as fire transforms old grief. I know just where to scatter the remains. Most of all, I know how to forgive. I'm starting now.

SISTERS AND OTHER STRANGERS

To the light of sisterhood—may it burn brightest in our darkest hours and never flicker in the winds of trial.

AUTHOR UNKNOWN

There were three sisters and two cousins who stood on the steps of the old Victorian house and posed for pictures right after World War II. Stairstep girls. All different. All brought up together in the same house by the various women who kept the home fires burning while the men were off to war.

Two of the sisters were convinced that they had enjoyed a wonderful childhood, replete with attention, discipline, love, manners, and lots and lots of relatives with laps and advice. But one sister, from the moment she was born, and even before, in the womb, or so she said, felt that she had been cheated, felt that she had been wronged. She had to find someone to blame. She blamed me.

It's hard to love someone when you are being judged by them. But sisters are forever, and so my other sister and my cousins have tried, over a space of almost sixty years, to understand. To love and to accept and to understand.

Recently there was a family wedding and a family reunion and all the sisters came together for a slumber party. How we laughed and how we cried and how we reminisced, with the family albums spread around us like a feast. We explored old letters and old poems and old family legends. We looked together again and again at the picture of the stairstep girls.

My heart opened with love and gratitude, remembering my childhood and how two of the sisters and both cousins all slept in the attic of the three-storey house during the war years, and left the lower two floors for the grownups. (My littlest sister slept downstairs with our mother, because she was so tiny.) I remember that there were holes in the pine floorboards where we could listen at night to the sound of the grownups' voices, if we had a mind to.

One of my sisters, who has been gifted in adulthood with a loving husband, a huge, close-knit family, money, health, slenderness, travel, possessions, and an assured old age of comfort, security, and wealth, began to share with us her childhood memories. No, there were no revelations of child abuse. No horrors, no nightmares. Just a raging dissatisfaction and scatter-shots of blame.

I wanted to listen. I wanted to understand. I wanted to be a part of her healing. But it tasted more like poison to me. It felt all spoiled. This weekend which had started out to be so promising had turned to ashes in my mouth. I wish it could have had a different ending. I wish I had not had to excuse myself and go to bed and toss and turn for hours, questioning the past and whatever part each of us had played in that past to make a mature woman so unhappy.

And then it came to me. No, not more blame. In fact, I said to myself then, and will say to my sister someday, when she does not seem so fragile, "I am not to blame for your childhood." That is a truth I know and she does not.

The memory that came to me was not of two little girls quarreling or becoming so different in adulthood that they find it almost impossible to communicate. The image that came to me was of the sisters (the two that supposedly didn't get along) sleeping together in the same bed. In the summer, we would kick off the sheet and open the windows and let the bakery across the street waft its yeast-rising, cinnamon-and-raisin-bread smell into every nook and cranny of the attic. We could hear the pans clatter and see the lights shining across the street all night long, when we were awake. But we usually slept the sweaty, deep sleep of children, safe, loved, cherished, peaceful children. In the winter, when the attic was icy, my little sister and I slept in long underwear, lying like two spoons cuddled together for warmth. Though we fought for the space heater fire as we dressed in the morning for school.

When we slept together, my little sister and I would breathe in the outbreath and then the inbreath of each other, and shift, and cough, and stir a little sometimes, but we would never let go of each other. We would sleep in the same bed and our breaths would mingle and our hands and arms and skinny legs would be wrapped around each other. We would not fight. We would, or so I remember, sleep peacefully and trustingly together, year after year. That is how I remember my childhood and the stairstep girls.

Perhaps someday my sister will remember it that way too. We'll come together in true celebration instead of ancient discontent. She will accept my love. She will accept me. And maybe love me too.

Pearls Before Swine

> *With enough sun and water to put down deep roots of self-esteem, children can withstand terrible storms. Without them, the slightest wind will seem full of danger.*

Gloria Steinem

$\mathcal{A}$ dear friend of mine tells me the story of her troubled granddaughter. The young woman in question is bright, beautiful, angry, rebellious, and acting out her unhappiness in self-destructive ways. My friend, terror in her heart, combined with exasperation and pity, cannot seem to reach her.

"What would you tell her if you could?" I ask her.

"I would put my hands on her shoulders and look into her eyes, and with all the force of my love, I would tell her, 'Don't throw your pearls before swine.' She wouldn't know what I mean, she wouldn't want to know what I mean. But somehow I would tell her."

"What could you tell her that she would hear?" I asked.

"That she has everything, when she thinks she has nothing. That she has youth and strength and brains and energy and a stubborn determination that, if harnessed properly, will take her far. I would tell her that seventeen is too young to give up, or run away, or court danger and disease by promiscuity. I would beg her not to kill herself, as she has tried before. That childhood hurts do not have to stop her life before it even starts. I would tell her that she has a bright future, that there is money for her schooling, that she can be whatever she wants to be. But first she must stop flailing about like a tantrum child. First she must become quiet, and let herself listen to her own longings for life. I would tell her not to dissipate herself by throwing herself away. I would tell her to honor herself, to cherish herself, to hold a part of herself private, guarded, inviolate. I would tell her that she is worthwhile, not worthless. I would tell her that she is a woman of value. And that out of that valuing and cherishing and honoring of even a spark of life within her, she can find strength to say no and strength to say yes and know the difference between the saying and the doing. All these things I would tell her. And she would hear me."

"Who does she listen to?"

"Neither her mother nor her father nor her stepmother nor her stepfather," my friend replied. "She had a counselor for a while, but her mother said she didn't need to go anymore."

The bitterness of that statement falls between us.

"She's off on her own, in another town," my friend says frantically. "How can I reach her?"

"Send prayers." Of course. What grandmother has not prayed for protection on the path for her grandchildren? "Surround her with your love. There will come a time when you can say to her what needs to be said."

That time came. In the middle of the night, the call came. The grandmother rescued her granddaughter and brought her to her home. They talked, the grandmother with tough love and a steely resolve to make a day and a night count, the young girl defensive, depressed, angry, misunderstood, misunderstanding, at cross-purposes. But they talked. Then the young girl left for home, a bus ticket clutched in her hand.

"For now, she is all right," said my friend. "For now, she is going back to school. For now, she is stable."

"Did you tell her about the pearls before swine?" I asked her.

"She laughed in my face," said my friend. "She thought it was the most old-fashioned thing she had ever heard. But I'm glad I said it."

I'm glad she said it too. How many years does it take for women to learn that we, just as we are, whether poised on the threshold of life or mature survivors, are valuable? Maybe we have a mother or a grandmother to remind us, to shake us awake before we throw our bodies away, before we numb our minds, before we offer up our hearts on silver platters to the nearest comer, before we dissipate our very essence.

Do you have a granddaughter you can tell? Fly to her side. Hold her in your arms and whisper, "You are good and true and bright and beautiful. Honor yourself. Hold yourself high."

And say those words to yourself too, no matter your age or circumstances. Whisper to yourself again and again, no matter what the world says about you as a category, as a problem, as a despairing, angry, tantrum child. Say those words to yourself as the wolf beats at the door, and illness pushes at your defenses, and loneliness seeps into the corners of your brave and solitary heart.

"You are good and true and bright and beautiful. Honor yourself. Hold yourself high."

And never, ever again cast your pearls before swine.

ACTS OF GRATITUDE

I see myself in my friends and in the people I work with, not on Madison Avenue and certainly not in the movies. I look at my friends as we all crumble gracefully and find joy and power in that.

LACE JACKSON

Many of us have had years and years of Norman Rockwell Thanksgivings. We have cooked the turkeys, we have seated twenty or more at dinner, we have fed our families and our friends generously, we have held hands at table and sung our blessings and our thankfulness. Some of us have fed the homeless on Thanksgiving. Some of us have visited nursing homes or manned crisis hotlines or worked through the holidays. In a mature lifetime, there are many kinds of holidays.

Yesterday I celebrated Thanksgiving with a group of women friends. They were the nucleus, the core group, and others wandered in and out during the day, from grown children dashing from one Thanksgiving table to another to the eighty-three-year-old boyfriend-widower of a woman who had been alive the Thanksgiving before. Some of our families couldn't get there. An ice storm was brewing in the country, stalling one young couple in their tracks. Another woman's son, a policeman, had to work. Other family members were scattered, traveling. It didn't look like a traditional family Thanksgiving at all.

I sat at the kitchen table, in the midst of the hubbub of too many women cooking in a small space, and observed. Women from their late forties to middle sixties, come together to cook and serve. One is a wealthy rancher and world traveler. One has inherited a cement company which she runs as competently as she once counseled parents and children in a school. One is self-employed. One has been downsized again and again during the health care industry upheaval. Sensitive to a fault, she wonders aloud of her "failure" to find another job until two weeks before. She now works sixty hours a week in a doctor's office, and is grateful she can pay her rent. I assure her that I am proud of her, that she is a success, that I knew she would land on her feet. Another woman, a single parent with three teenage sons, will lose her home in a few months due to a divorce decree made many years ago.

We peel and mix and stir, sharing pictures of a recent family wedding, a trip to Mexico, new grandchildren. One high-strung friend, a perpetual motion machine, whirls around in a frenzy of preparations, mashing potatoes, making gravy, banging open cabinets, spilling flour and salt, stirring vegetables. She is a one-woman hurricane in another woman's kitchen. We gossip and laugh and tease her and stay out of the whirlwind. We share our stories. The eighty-three-year-old widower and the teenage boys watch football in the living room. The women have taken over the kitchen entirely, three of them having spent the night at my friend's house in order to cook the turkey and pies the night before.

Finally, when the smells of home cooking threaten to overwhelm us all, the dinner is done. We hold hands and say a blessing, remembering those who were with us the year before, and are now no more. With a final squeeze of hands, we welcome our feast. But what I am starved for is the female companionship, the nourishment stirred into mashed potatoes, the nurturing of home-baked pies, the kindness enveloped in each bite.

Each woman there has cooked thousands of meals, raised children, buried or divorced husbands, taken care of her parents, worked hard for a living. They are of differing faiths, differing financial circumstances, differing outlooks. Yet even while the sleet begins to hiss outside in an already-darkening sky, we come together. To feed ourselves and others. To bless ourselves and others. To remember our loved ones who are with us no more. To release our grown children to their own celebrations. To laugh together while the night presses in.

Before I went to my friend's house for this Thanksgiving, I called another woman friend to see how she was. She was facing her third surgery during the holidays, and I wanted to check on her. Truth to tell, I dreaded the call. How could I be of help? Holidays disarm my defenses. Memory rushes in uninvited, unwanted. There are all those Thanksgivings of the past, and all the people I loved who are no longer with me.

She answered the phone and I braced myself against her pain. But she was joyful. "I woke up this morning," she told me, "and I felt like the luckiest woman in the world. My children are coming to give me what they call 'a Waltons' Thanksgiving, traditional as all get-out. I don't even have to get out of bed. They are all coming. They are all giving to me.

"I feel so grateful," she said, this gallant, skinny, pretty woman who has struggled for years with ill health. "I want to make an Act of Gratitude. Today I am thanking God for all the good that is in my life." We talk for a little while, and when I hang up the phone, I say "Thank you" out loud. Then I go on to my friend's house, bearing my cranberry apple pie.

You know the rest. We gathered together. We laughed and cried and ate too much, and bore goodwill offerings home for another feast. I was the first one to leave. I am not the best of drivers in the best of times, and the rain and the dark waited. But I was full of light. I was full of hope. I was full of thanksgiving. And so I made an Act of Gratitude as I made my way homeward, remembering the blessings of this homey gathering of gallant women. Listening to one another. Helping each other. Feeding each other. For all this and more I give thanks.

GIFTS FOR THE GUESTS

I always felt that the great high privilege, relief and comfort of friendship was that one had to explain nothing.

KATHERINE MANSFIELD

$\mathcal{A}$t a birthday party for a friend of mine named Lynda who had just turned fifty, the honoree took the time, after food and talk and presents and before the creative gifts of entertainment we all presented to her (most of the guests were in creative fields), to go around the circle and to express to each one of us aloud what her perceptions of us were, and how we had first come into her life and then enriched her life with the gift of our presence. There were about thirty women at the party. Many of us were strangers to each other. It took a long time to acknowledge each of us. It was worth it.

So often, as an older woman in this society, I think to myself that I, and only I, know that I am of worth, of value, of strength, of courage. I matter.

As does each woman I meet, each in their own individual, unique, valuable way. But we seldom tell each other. And we seldom tell ourselves. Women of my generation, especially, were not taught to put themselves forward. "It is not seemly to repeat compliments about yourself," I was told as a child by numerous female relatives who undertook to tame my exuberance and make me more docile and ladylike. So even as I write this essay, I quail inside to think that I could ever be repeating compliments about myself. It's just not done! What ever will you think of me?

This is what my birthday friend told the assembled guests. She called me "a creative spitfire who had come into her life with the power of words." She called me an elegant and earthy writer with words that wound their way into her heart and mind and said what she wanted to say about her own life. She said she wished that she had written just one of my books. She said she cherished me and my wisdom.

As my lovely friend continued around the circle, dropping words of kindness into other women's famished hearts, I sat there mute, my face scarlet, sinuses stuffed, tears threatening to overflow.

What did she mean? I hadn't been called a spitfire since adolescence, when I refused to put out for an acne-covered teenager who wanted to wrestle with me in the back seat of his father's Studebaker. What did she mean? Of course I'm creative, that's my job, for God's sake, but what was all the rest? Didn't she know that I was really an old mule, an aging workhorse, a beast of burden? Didn't she know of current disappointments and past tragedies? Of years of caregiving, intermingled with years of poverty? Who was this woman she saw? And what had *that* woman to do with me?

I was a plump, middle-aged woman. How could I be elegant and earthy? And both at the same time? I wished for wisdom, but seldom acknowledged its entrance into my life and into my words on the page. She must have the wrong woman, I decided. I'd call her the next day and thank her and set her straight.

I never did. Because I got to thinking that maybe, just maybe, she saw something in me that I had hidden, covered over, dismissed, or, conversely, longed for but never attained (especially the stuff about my writing). Maybe her perceptions were valid after all. Maybe I could let my natural energy out a little more playfully. Spitfire! Who knew? Maybe I could begin to think of myself in a more elegant and earthy way. Maybe the wisdom I sought was all around me and within me, and maybe a little of that same energy could and would and did flow into the words I wrote on the page, words telling other women how wonderful and magical and valuable they are.

I noticed then how each woman opened like a flower when my friend told all those gathered of that particular woman's strength and goodness. What fascinating women we all were! I longed to know each one better. I did, through my friend's words to them and about them. I related to them all, once they were introduced to me by my friend's gift of kind words. From the elderly Baptist Sunday-school teacher, to the young opera singer, the well-known harpist, the bookstore owner, the voice professor, the anthropologist from New Mexico, the long-time Texas neighbor come all the way from Arizona, the woman missionary, the artist from Germany, the young mother, and the retired professor. Thirsty for praise, open to receive. How we blossomed, how we shone!

Sometimes other people's perceptions are cruel or dismissive, and almost always inaccurate. But sometimes! Ah sometimes! There comes an evening of epiphanies, when the full moon rides high above the acres around a large and hospitable house in the Texas countryside, full of feast and friendship, full of music and dance and song and full expression, where women come together, not only to celebrate a birthday but to celebrate each other.

And I was there, all elegant, earthy, creative spitfire wisdom of me. I was there! And I took home the gift of me.

I Found a Million-Dollar Baby

It is good to have an end to journey toward, but it is the journey that matters, in the end.

URSULA K. LE GUIN

Once I wanted to write a short story about my Aunt Betty, whose life, on the surface, looked so tragic. My aunt was a bouncy, smart, sunshiny youngest daughter. During World War II she worked outside the home as a single woman and was, to my eight-year-old eyes, a glamorous career woman. Her boyfriend during that time sent her a cardboard cutout picture of herself, from one he had taken earlier. It was mounted on some kind of plywood, so that the woman in the picture stood erect and smiling on the mantelpiece. Underneath it he had written, "I found my million-dollar baby in a five-and-ten-cent store."

Now, for those of you who do not remember the World War II songs, this was a national hit that had us all humming. Who among us did not harbor dreams of being "discovered" by a war hero, while clerking in the five-and-dime? It was the stuff that movies were made of, in that day and time.

Alas, my aunt's boyfriend did not come back from the war. She continued to work outside the home, but lived at home dutifully and frugally, among the household of ten females that survived the war years together. She went to secretarial school, got a pin that said she had graduated, and supported herself working for the oil and gas industry. She met a man, a rather exotic man named Sam, who had a Cajun name and a Louisiana past. They married. Her first son, Tom, was born prematurely, retarded and blind from too much oxygen given him at birth to save his life. Her third son died of AIDS in the early days of the epidemic, before anyone even knew the name of the disease. Only her second son, who became a dentist, survived. Long before that, my aunt's husband, he of the dashing name and oilfield work, died and left her a young widow.

My aunt and I shared some time together when my niece got married. By then, time and grief and too much alcohol had taken its toll on her. We talked for hours in the corner of the room, while preparations for the wedding bustled around us. She tried to explain to me why she drank. "It's my only friend," she explained carefully. "Everyone and everything I loved, except for my remaining son, has gone from me." She lived alone in a small apartment with her cats for company. She worked now in a dry-cleaning shop, the only job she could get after alcohol rehab. But during that weekend of the wedding, when the owner of the shop gave her time off, she told me her story. We laughed and cried together. When my niece walked down the aisle in her white wedding dress, just like in all the fairy tales, my aunt and I looked at one another with heartbreak in our eyes. We did not need to say aloud what each of us experienced at that moment. There is no happily ever after. We held each other's hands and cried. Then she went back to work. Or so we thought.

When my aunt failed to arrive for work, the owner of the shop finally located her surviving son. He and one of my sons broke down the door to her apartment. My aunt had hit her head on the corner of a table. She must have been drinking heavily. She lay there suffering from a cerebral hemmorhage. She died alone.

But when I remember my aunt and her life, I remember her like this. She once was young. She was an independent woman, in days when women were seldom so. She was once a young man's dream. She was his "million-dollar baby found in a five-and-ten-cent store." She had a husband, three children, and years of possibilities before the sad ending of her story. That's just the point. She had a story. She had a life to tell me. She mattered.

Perhaps you will not think that my aunt had a long or fulfilling life. No matter. She had a journey. Her lessons were those of loss, but they were also lessons of survival. Right to the very end she kept her sense of humor, even in the face of adversity. We had those moments of connection, at a family wedding. Whenever I think of how she met her end, I will remember her as dashing and sunshiny, smiling from a mantelpiece, while a young man crooned a love song to her. I will remember her as a million-dollar woman.

OTHER PEOPLE'S CHOICES

*"There's no accounting for tastes," said the old woman
as she kissed the cow.*

ANONYMOUS

$\mathcal{I}$'ve heard that story since I was a child, and it just goes to
show that (1) the mind retains the oddest truisms and (2)
thank goodness we are not all alike!

Sometimes it seems to me that the whole idea of demo-
graphics bears no relationship to the differentnesses we share,
no matter our age or geographical location.

My dear friend Alicia is one example—an exuberant,
ample Hispanic woman. We have known each other since
clear back in college (both with children, putting ourselves
through), and then worked together for a year in a Federal Job
Skills Training program, where I introduced her to the man
she later married (our boss). In the intervening twenty-five
years or so, Alicia raised her children and went back to school
again and became a school counselor, as well as teaching English as a Second Language at night. When I came back from
my sojourn in L.A., we renewed our friendship.

Last week I went to see Alicia and her now eighty-year-
old husband at their new house. It was in a new subdivision,

way out from the city, one-and two-storey model homes of brick and frame, with winding sidewalks and young trees. Lots of children scooting around, lots of young, hopeful families. The wind blew in off the prairie and the children ran shrieking from house to house. People were putting in new grass and barbecuing outdoors. A curious feeling of déjà vu assaulted my senses. Surely this was another Texas city, farther west, and surely it was *my* children starting school. Surely it was the bland and optimistic 1950s, where Father knew best and housewives still wore print dresses, where the concern was over waxy buildup rather than street gangs. Where everything was new and fresh and clean and unmarked. Everything was possible, and everything and everyone was the same.

Alicia had moved in just a week earlier. She knew the bricklayers who stopped by her house to visit with her. She invited the head of the sales force for the subdivision in, when he stopped by to pick up the bricklayer. She showed him around, how everything fit, how perfect it all was. Alicia chattered to one visitor in Spanish, to another in English, offering coffee and advice all at once. Grandchildren swooped in (they live just two blocks away), and new neighbors (she already knew everyone) dropped in for coffee. The phone never stopped ringing.

She showed us all the features and the accomodations. Wider doorways, so that when her husband went to a wheelchair she could maneuver him easily through the house. A handicapped ramp sloping down to the street from the garage, so that she could walk him around the neighborhood. His hobby room set up first, with his ham radio system and western novels, and his easy chair, so that he could be comfortable.

"Best of all, the grandchildren walk right past my house to and from school," Alicia exclaimed. "So I'm always here for them, especially when their parents are working." She had retired early from the school system, two years ago, in order to care for her new granddaughter, who by now is too big for Alicia to lug around. Her parents are elderly and her father cantankerous and often ill. Her mother will probably move close to her at a later date.

I look past the beige carpeting, the white walls, the small and boxy bedrooms. Not my style. Not my taste. Not my life. But how wonderful to be so enthusiastic, so loving, so situated that when family calls, you are there. Alicia is the epicenter of her family. She is earth mother, caregiver, and every cliché of grandmother that we grew up with.

"I've come so far," she exults. She has. She confided to me once about her early beginnings, raised in a downtown slum over a bar. She was the first woman in her family to get a divorce (many years ago, with three children to raise). She was the first woman in her family to get a college degree, and then a master's degree, and then a teaching certificate, and then another master's degree, this one in counseling. She started her own translation business. She has traveled widely. She has gone far and wide and away from her beginnings. And now? Now she is the quintessential grandmother, living out every TV dream she watched when she was younger.

I am bemused by other people's choices. I celebrate my friend's happiness. I suggest a housewarming. But is there any need for that at all? Alicia, by her very presence, makes her house warm.

Risk! Risk anything! Care no more for the opinion of others, for those voices. Do the hardest thing on earth for you. Act for yourself. Face the truth.

KATHERINE MANSFIELD

I have a friend who grew up in the heartland in the '40s and '50s. Since then she has watched the rules and expectations for women change with each decade. Oh, she knew who she was. A giver, a nurturer, a wife, a mother, a daughter, a teacher, a single-parent provider for a while. A survivor. She was college-educated. She was smart. She had that peculiar blend of stoicism and stamina that got her through. From giving birth to facing death, to love and loss and hanging in there and all points in between. Along the way she met and married a brilliant, charming, difficult, potentially life-enhancing but ultimately self-destructive man. She stayed almost twenty years too long.

The end came one day with a whimper of rage and a clunk, like croquet balls rolling around inside your head and then ultimately settling in the pit of your stomach.

In the midst of a discussion that threatened to turn into a firestorm if pursued to its end, her husband turned to her and said dismissively, "At least, with me, you've never missed a meal." And the woman saw twenty years of feeding others—children, parents, friends, and yes, the husband—reduced to that one telling phrase. "At least, by staying with me, you've never missed a meal."

"When I heard that phrase," she told me, "my heart went cold. Because I had fed *him*. All he had done was pay for the groceries."

Yet to sum up a lifetime, a marriage, in that one phrase—"I have fed you"—told her as much about herself and her gradual dependence upon a man as it told her the truth about the man she loved. A lifetime reduced to the fear implicit behind those words.

For the woman saw then that whether she was being told to stay home or go to work, get an education or remain barefoot and pregnant, whether she was told that she couldn't, oughtn't, shouldn't, mustn't—get her Ph.D. or get a promotion, follow her vision or cancel her dream, defer to her husband or obey an Old Testament God who thundered punishment from a white cloud, all—all!—were outside messages. Ingrained, instilled, ingested from a bitter and tender age. If the sum of who she was—all she was!—strengths and weaknesses, heroic acts and everyday decisions, magnificent and tireless nurturing—if all she could say at the end of it all was "I have never missed a meal"—What did that say *about* her? *to* her?

We are bombarded with contrary and useless messages that find no congruency within our hearts and souls. You *know* these messages. You inhaled them with your mother's milk. You learned them at your father's knee. These messages say: "You are limited. You are not enough. You need someone else, a father, a husband, a lover, a boss, a grandfather God, to take care of you. You cannot make it on your own. You can feed others. But you cannot feed yourself. You must be both strong and weak at the same time."

And so, whether you are thirty-five or forty-five or fifty-five, you hold that fear, that self-doubt inside you. It is reinforced within and without by a thousand messages. It has nothing to do with ability or worth. It has to do with perception.

No matter what a woman's outer reality shows her, no matter if she is capable and confident and has a few bucks in the bank, she—you—we—are filled with poverty messages. We can be smart, we can be tireless, we can do it all (or almost all), but it is never enough. *We* are never enough. We give and give and give some more. We try harder. We run in place. We start over. We grow older. We become invisible. What then? Where and when did we miss the signals? The changing choices? Oh dreams denied, deferred, or feared! What next? What now?

One day, usually midlife or a bit after (aren't we late bloomers all?), we come face to face with that pervasive self-doubt, that corroding and uniquely feminine fear. Unnurtured, malnourished, unprovided for, we feel in the inner deep of our belly (at gut level) how we have traded approval for a meal, how we have "made nice," how we have pleased and performed and made ourselves over into whatever current fleeting image is dictated by the fluctuating fashions and fortunes, mores and morality, of current culture.

Until we are empty. Until there is only a ghost in the mirror, a shadow on the stairs. Until we must, at some point, say, "Stop. No more." Until we shakily, tentatively, secretly, begin to fill the caverns of need waiting and watching within us. Until we give to ourselves as well as to others. Until we respect and acknowledge ourselves. Until the worm has turned. Until the game is over. Until the truth is told. Until we take care of ourselves as bountifully and as compassionately and as generously as we have others. Until we face the fear, face the self-doubt, and vow to go through it and beyond it. Until we pledge to feed *ourselves.* Until we are fed.

What starts as sticks and stones and crusts of bread and handouts from others can come—will come!—as a banquet, a feast, a thanksgiving.

Oh, and my friend, the one whose husband summed up their married life with "You've never missed a meal." She left him. Of course she did. Reader, what else do you *think* she could do?

And she has never missed a meal since then. Not ever. She is fearless. And she is fed.

THE WELL-MARRIED WOMAN

No, I don't understand my husband's theory of relativity, but I know my husband and I know he can be trusted.

ELSA EINSTEIN

$\mathcal{E}$very morning when I walk my path through the labyrinth of interlocking courts overlooking the park, I smile and nod and say good morning to an elderly couple who walk the same curving streets. She has to be at least eighty years old, and almost blind, as she clutches onto the arm of her somewhat younger husband and lets him lead her, shuffling step by shuffling step, around one street to another. He matches his steps to hers, and calls out to passersby. I envy them.

My grandmother would have called them "well married." This is a phrase from her generation, usually referring to a "well-married woman," as one who had managed, through grace or guile, through fortune or favor, to marry well—that is, to marry a man who would provide well for her and any children they might have, and ensure her place in a social hierarchy of southern culture, and oh, by the way, someone who would love and cherish her over many years. How times have changed!

I know several well-married women. A few have been married thirty or forty years or more. Length of time, however, does not ensure a well marriage. Wasn't it Carol Burnett who, on being asked why her marriage of twenty years had "failed," said that she did not consider twenty good years a failure at all, but rather a success for both of them?

I have several friends who are widows. They were well-married women once. Does this make them less so, just because their beloved husbands have gone on before them? Divorce is no arbiter of whether a woman is or has been well married, either. Sometimes time is the culprit, and quality outshines quantity. But I know what my grandmother means. In an uncertain world, and growing older by the minute, who among us, as we age, has not wished, at one time or another, to be loved and cherished, safe and secure and well-provided for?

Usually it's the women who take care of the men, especially as we grow older and hardier. So I mark even more carefully the couple who walk together daily and are well married for a lifetime.

Such was not my choice. I was married for over thirty years of my life, through two long and difficult marriages. I can remember the few years when I felt like a well-married woman. Most of the time I did not.

Truth to tell, being well married is seldom an option for the mature women that I know. Especially since it takes two to tango. And two to stay well married, through every turn of time and fortune. So if you are or have been in the past a well-married woman, I am glad for you. Everyone deserves a little love in a lifetime. But if you are no longer a well-married woman, that's all right too. No failures here, only a long life of experiences of love, in whatever shape or form they take.

You have loved long and well, no matter the result. I mark your passage. And wish you love again before you die.

Mind Radiant

Reading,
Writing,
Creating,
Dreaming,
and the
'Rithmetic
Of Wealth

MIND RADIANT

We tend to identify thoughts and feelings with the mind, thinking they are the whole of the mind, when they are truly only the surface of the mind. Our minds are naturally clear, deep, and spacious, like the sky. Our thoughts and feelings are like clouds floating through that sky. And in the space between thoughts, the radiant nature of the mind shines through.

DIANE MARIECHILD

$\mathcal{I}$ was watching a show on PBS about the brain and expected to see and hear the ways in which as we grow older our minds atrophy, harden, dim, decline. I was intrigued enough to listen as one talking head explained to another that even though we lose billions of brain cells as we grow older, an interesting and remarkable thing happens to our brain. One doctor called it synthesis. One scientist called it crystallized wisdom. I call it the radiant nature of the mind.

Imagine, if you will, that all you have ever learned, felt, seen, heard, tasted, smelled, loved, hated is stored in your brain just waiting for the right time to be used. To be brought forth. Crystallized wisdom. Dendrites and synapses making connections, flashing their way like crystal points of light from one cell to another, giving directions, making new connections. Synthesizing years of knowledge into a coherent and beautiful whole. Sure beats joking to a friend as you forget your keys, "Oh God, it must be Alzheimer's." Not a joking matter, ever!

It just goes to show that earlier assumptions can be changed. We don't have to lose our minds as we grow older. We can, through lots of exercise of those brain cells, keep the connections flowing, synthesize what we have learned. Just as a muscle exercised patiently again and again to its full potential will work better and keep its tone and strength better, so too will your mind as you exercise it.

Imagine if you will a supple, sinuous mind that grasps new concepts. Imagine if you will a vital mind that solves problems easily. Imagine a mind that can cut to the heart of the matter and offer clear solutions. Imagine if you will a mind that enjoys and resonates with the written word and the spoken word, playing with language as you once played with toys. Imagine a mind that evolves constantly, even as the world is evolving. Imagine a mind that can create and then crystallize the thought forms into a new invention. Imagine a mind that sings. Imagine a mind that rejoices. Radiant mind!

You can train your mind with everything from crossword puzzles to classical music to conflict resolution. You can memorize poetry and chant it to yourself. You can walk in rhythm with the flow of words and watch how the mind makes a pattern of the words. You can meditate and watch how over time the mind lets go of jumpiness and distress and smooths into a flow of energy. You can follow a thought back to its source and catch a glimpse of just how your mind makes a path, jumps to another path, and weaves erratically from thought to thought. You can focus and discipline your mind so that it does not scatter into fragments. You can train your mind before you go to sleep at night to work with you throughout the night for creative problem-solving. You can let your mind drift and dream upon awakening, like rocking in a hammock, until the soft music of its movements leads you to peaceful discoveries. You can learn to let go of the mind, drop it into a pool of stillness, and then observe how it returns unto its center. All these things and more you can do for the continued health of your mind.

I can remember when there was so-called scientific evidence (read generally accepted conventional thought) that women, supposedly because their heads were smaller, were incapable of reasoning, creating, inventing, or any kind of sustained and logical thought. My mother's and my grandmother's generations were exposed to this kind of prejudice, and in many ways so was my generation. Now we would find this laughable, if it were not so demeaning. I know women who have waited until every male in their household was grown and gone before they dared to burst forth in a spurt of learning that took them to new heights of pleasure and of competence. I know women who thrive at elderhostels or return to universities for advanced degrees because now, finally, their intellectual flowering can burst forth. Oh discriminating, discerning, well-used, zealous minds!

Begin now. Pick up any book and there's the start of lifetime learning. Take classes, especially any you can find that seek to harmonize the mind with the body, the mind with the emotions, the mind with the spirit. Oh what a lifetime you have left to synthesize and crystallize your wisdom. Dynamic mind. Radiant mind.

Shabby Underwear and All Things Unloving

> *Gratification is the filling of your containers. When you are dissatisfied with your life, examine your containers, but look also at your ability to allow them to fill.*
>
> Ellen Meredith

I swore I'd never trash another writer in print, no matter how much I disagreed with his or her premises. We're here to help each other, aren't we? While I do have to be discerning as I review upwards of two hundred books a year, still I try my best not to be ugly. But I am incensed, offended, and outraged by a book that came across my desk the other day. It purports to help older women. It doesn't.

Among the pluses of living alone and growing older, according to the author, is that one can wear shabby underwear or not even bother to *change* one's underwear. There's much more, from riding the bus all day if you are lonely in order to make friends (whatever happened to volunteer work?), to buying Salvation Army pieces of cloth and cutting a hole in them and making blouses for yourself, to sneaking into medical conventions to get freebies and sneaking into luxury hotels to swim free.

Now please believe me when I say that the author does not write this book in a tongue-in-cheek way. This is no parody of aging women. She is earnest. She is sincere. This is real advice. I hate it.

Where (except in the pages of this and perhaps a few other misguided books) is it written that we have to be poor, alone, unloved, shabby? Where is it written that we have to make do, be less, be limited, be cunning thieves in order to steal aspirin or adult diapers or a dip in a hotel pool? Why should we? How demeaning. How futile.

For if we make ourselves less than we are, if, in the name of either excessive frugality or clever cheating (read medical conventions or hotel pools), we either do without or sneak our way, unpaid, unasked, into a life we think we are not entitled to, then we diminish ourselves. By such acts, piled day by day and year by year upon each other, we create a monster that yearns for more and settles for less. We perpetuate our sense of being not enough. We declare ourselves lacking and less than.

I wish that someone, a wealthy friend, a compassionate relative, would treat this author to a spa vacation and some new clothes. Especially new underwear. Three-packs of long-lasting white cotton panties are $5.99 at Montgomery Wards. Probably the same in her neck of the woods too.

Of course you are not going to follow her advice. But take a minute. Look around you. In what ways are you limiting yourself? In what ways are you thriftily unloving? Make a list. You'd be surprised. Throw out or give away all that is shabby in your life. It will make room for new. It will make room for you.

Then pay your own way. You can swim at the Y if you can't afford a luxury vacation. You can buy generic brands instead of misrepresenting yourself at a medical convention. A library card will get you most books, if you can't afford the latest bestseller. But there's a huge difference between frugality and lack. Self-respect. *That's* what I call it.

And treat yourself to some new underwear while you're about it. You're worth it.

A Chair for My Lover

> *Thought that is no longer limited, brings experience that is no longer limited.*
>
> MARIANNE WILLIAMSON

$\mathcal{Y}$ears ago, I wrote some articles for a regional magazine and in the process met the new editor-in-chief of the magazine. We became friends for a while, until I moved away and the magazine folded. I have not thought of her for years. Until now.

Are you familiar with the oversized, overstuffed, green-and-white-cotton-covered reading chairs in some Barnes & Noble bookstores? You know, the ones you can curl up into for a moment or two to scan a magazine or a new book you might buy and then, losing yourself in the text, sink deeper into the chair until more time than you realize has passed? Just like sinking into an old-fashioned easy chair in your own home. I know. I have one patterned in almost the same fabric, but yellow with green sprigs, in my bedroom.

My editor friend and I went out for dinner one night before I left my hometown for greener pastures, and her story spilled out over Chinese food. About the divorce she had gone through, and the uprootedness she had experienced when she moved across the country, and how she found her current job and current condo and started over, all alone, in a strange town far from her roots. How scared she was. How she wondered every day of her working life how she would make it in a new job, in a new city, all alone. How she wanted a friend. How she wanted a man. How she wanted a lover. And she didn't quite know how to get any or all of the above.

"Well, I am your friend," I pointed out to her, "as you are mine. The rest will come." So we started brainstorming as to how she could make her life happier.

Later, she sent me a photograph. It was a picture of a large, green-and-white, overstuffed, oversized easy chair. With it was a note. "I bought this on the advice of a friend," she wrote. "It's sitting in my living room. No one sits in it. It's waiting for my wonderful man to come along. It's for him. Every night I imagine him sitting in it across from me. It's a chair for my lover."

I wrote back to her. "Let me know when he comes along." Then thought no more about it.

A few months later, I received another note and another picture. My friend, who is short and squat and plump, was posed next to a younger man, tall, thin, dark, and pleasant-looking. He was sitting—you guessed it—in the green-and-white easy chair and my friend was standing next to him, one arm curved over the chair back and around the man. They were both grinning as if they had won the lottery.

"We're going to be married," she wrote. "He's moving in while he finishes his residency." A doctor, no less! "I'm so happy," she went on. "P.S. The chair worked!"

I love happy endings. And such a delicious story. To think that a chair could attract to it the fulfillment of a friend's prayer.

So every time I go into Barnes & Noble and sink down into *their* easy chairs, I think of my friend and her lover. And laugh aloud for a moment, so that the other people around me look up from their magazines for an instant. Those chairs, of course, contain the daily imprint of many people's energy. Not likely, then, that a very special person would gravitate next to my adjoining chair.

But I *do* happen to have that cottony yellow-and-green-print chair in my bedroom. No one's used it but me. Only my energy enfolds it. I could, I suppose, project longing and designate it as a chair for my lover. Who? Not likely. Probably unwise. Hardly possible. Foolish dream. You have to want something or someone enough to make it happen. And yet. And just suppose. Nah. Never happen. It was my friend's dream, not mine. I'm just glad it came true.

BAG LADY BLUES

You gain strength, courage, and confidence by every experience in which you really stop to look fear in the face. . . . You must do the thing you think you cannot do.

ELEANOR ROOSEVELT

When I visited friends in San Francisco a couple of years ago, we sat around the table talking and laughing late into the night, while the food got cold and the candles guttered, while the dreams and the fears of each of us came forth to be dissected and discussed. I was visiting a colleague who lived in a magnificent house on three levels, with a view of the bay. She had earned this house and her profession (she is CEO of her own company) on her own. She and the other women who shared our evening were younger than I, smart, well-educated, hardworking, professional. Each had more energy than I think I will ever have again.

Somehow the discussion turned to money and worth and future expectations. And a beautiful and clever woman of about fifty, with her own legal practice, shared with us her deepest fear. "I'm afraid that I will end up a bag lady, old, alone, penniless, crazy," she shivered. "I guess that's my worst and most irrational fear."

The rest of us nodded our heads in rueful acceptance. "I don't know a woman over fifty, maybe even younger, who hasn't felt that way at one time or another," we each chimed in. We tried to turn it into a joke, but there had been too many sleepless nights for each of us pondering just such a fate.

"I know," I said. "I'll write a book about it and call it *The Feminine Face of Fear.*" I wrote the following passage instead.

BAG LADY BLUES

I'm living on 10 percent of what I made in L.A. Go figure. This is the '90s. Not that I'm stuck in any category of mobility. I've been up and I've been down. It's all relative. Change happens. I'll be up again. It's inevitable. But once in a while I get the mean red—low-down—woe is me!—bag lady blues.

I'll bet you do too, if you are a woman of a certain age and generation and not being supported by either a trust fund or a man. Now I know that sounds sexist, since we make our own reality, and we make our own luck, and God helps those who help themselves, but in this day and age, and with all the downsizing of companies, and the old and the unskilled, and the last-hired first-fired, and the trading in for newer models, and the sheer tough longevity of women everywhere, I'll bet you too, once in a while, get the mean red—low-down—woe is me!—bag lady blues.

Of course poverty is not limited to women, but they get a discount on it and the lion's share of it. And if you're alone, and middle-aged or elderly, and female, and self-employed, and in an artistic field, sometimes you get the mean red—low-down—woe is me!—bag lady blues.

Sometimes freelance means you give away your work for free, or get paid late, or less, or not at all, and hardly ever what you're worth. But you get clever and tough and hardy, and the more someone else, anyone else, tells you you can't survive, the more you do. Even on those days and nights when you get the mean red—low-down—woe is me!—bag lady blues.

I have several female friends who are writers or painters or dancers or actors. They manage. They create. They make do. They continue.

One friend of mine, who is a writer, told me with wonder in her voice of a male acquaintance of hers, much younger, an assistant college professor, who, when he lost his job, felt such a failure that he killed himself.

Suicide, of course, is not limited to gender, age, race, or education. Failure happens in the eye of the beholder. We've all been there. I have. So have you. But couldn't he have gotten another job, any job, and continued with his life, learning from adversity, and all that? Surely he was more than the classes he taught? Surely he was more than his name in a college catalog? There must have been more to his pain than we will ever know. But still. It happened in a sunny town where the living is easy, and most people can get unemployment compensation. My friend couldn't figure it out, even though she, like you and me, has lain awake at night wondering how to continue in the uncertain, ambiguous career path she has chosen.

Maybe it was the sheer terror of living without a net or a network. We'll never know. But my friend the writer continues to scrape by. Eight books published, plus a few hundred articles. She can almost live on her royalties, with editing jobs on the side.

I admire her and I understand her, but she is not unique. She's just like you and me. We choose every day—every day!—to follow our dream, follow our talent, follow our bliss. We choose to discover who we are from every experience, from every job, from every person. We learn from our failures and we are amazed and astonished and grateful and vindicated by our successes. We live fully. We live freely.

I asked my friend what she would do if it ever came to being that bag lady with the shopping cart. It is her nightmare too. "I'd write about it," she said. "I'd use it."

"But it won't come to that," we tell ourselves bravely. We laugh and meet once a year for a budget lunch. "Because we are the lucky ones. We turn everything we are into words on a page. We're smart, we're educated, we're talented."

We are the heroes of our own lives. All of that is true.

And yet. We're alone. We're aging. We're almost broke. We endure.

And so, once in a while, we both get the mean red—lowdown—woe is me!—bag lady blues.

A Woman's Wealth

*Often people attempt to live their lives backwards: they
try to have more things, or more money, in order to do
more of what they want so that they will be happier.
The way it actually works is the reverse. You must
first be who you really are, then do what you need to do,
in order to have what you want.*

MARGARET YOUNG

I've been rich and I've been poor and awareness is better. That's not sour grapes. It is a measured evaluation that I can feel from my head to my toes, that tells me that I do enough, I have enough, and I *am* enough.

A friend of mine who is a minister in L.A. told me once that she discovered one day that she owned sixty silk blouses and that she was still dissatisfied. "How can anyone ever wear sixty silk blouses?" she asked. Later she gave most of them away.

I decided then and there that if wealth was really what I wanted, the wealth I sought would be in the flow of ideas, not in the sheer accumulation of things. My friend, like me, was an ardent metaphysician, but she had never believed, and neither do I, that walking around like a zombie and muttering to yourself one hundred times a day, "I am rich, I am rich, I am rich," accomplished anything at all except in the noticing, day by day, of what wasn't working, of what was lacking, or of how far to go before words became reality.

When I owned my own small company in L.A., I got a wonderful chance to see how the inflow and outflow of money and ideas really worked. It was a valuable learning experience for me. When business cycles changed, when the economy of southern California collapsed, when expansion became contraction, I was not wise enough to see then that this was in the natural order of things. I only knew that I had to get back to my roots in my old hometown and reground myself in the safety and the values I had learned there. These values had come from my own grandmother, she of the indomitable will, who, as a poverty-stricken widow from a once-wealthy family, had supported ten women and girls during World War II.

This is not an apology for not having. It is an assessment of what wealth really means. I felt for years that I was a failure because I couldn't make the universe give me what I wanted, when I wanted it. Sort of like a child crying for the moon. I had to learn that who I am is more important than what I possess, before the flow of wealth could find its way to me again.

I believe that real wealth is in the currency of ideas. What other way to explain how year after year, decade after decade, I make my living by arranging words on paper to express emotions and ideas? What is the price of a word? What is the value of a story? How many books will I sell this year? But I digress.

I believe that the wealth of women offers much to the

world, in ways that we do not notice or comment on. Invisible underpinnings of a society focused on the outer trappings. For most women it is not "The one with the most toys wins," but rather, "What can I do that makes a difference in the world?" What kind of a person can I be, so that my children learn right from wrong, so that my family feels loved and cared for, so that my community is safe, so that the elderly are nurtured, so that the disenfranchised do not fall through the cracks? What can I contribute, how can I serve? In business, in church, in community, in schools, in the service sector, we ask ourselves and follow through with deeds as well as words. I do not need sixty silk blouses or a new car every year to ask the questions or to follow through with action. Awareness serves me and others more than greed.

And when the fear comes (and it will!) of who will take care of *me* when I am old, who will take care of *me* if I am ill or impoverished—what then? Those of us who have learned the lessons of ups and downs and expansion and contraction can know, then, that we *are* enough. That inner wealth will support us. And that outer wealth, in whatever its current manifestation, will follow.

As for me, I have an old, beautiful, serene house, filled with family memories. I have more books than I can ever read (I recycle constantly), and I have the tools of my trade, from computer and laser printer to paper and pens. I have friends and family and good work. More and more, as the years go by, I trust in the universe to provide for me. As I provide for others. As for the currency of ideas, there is no shortage here. Ideas are infinite. That's wealth! As my awareness grows, my words bear fruit. And I am satisfied.

AGELESS CREATIVITY

But goals are not meant to be heavy insights on your spirit. They are stars to navigate by. And gratification is not a prize to win at the end of a long struggle. It is something to experience as you inhabit each moment.

ELLEN MEREDITH

One of my favorite writers, Harriet Doerr, gave me this, in her writing: "I have everything I need. A square of sky, a piece of stone, a page, a pen, and memory raining down on me in sleeves."

Harriet Doerr was born in 1910. She graduated from Stanford University with a B.A. in 1977 when she was in her sixties. Her first novel, *Stones for Ibarra,* was published when she was seventy-five. It won the National Book Award in 1984 and garnered a host of other prizes, secured her grants and fellowships, and was made into a movie. Her second novel, *Consider This, Señora,* published when she was in her eighties, was also highly praised, widely read, and at least on my part, deeply cherished.

Now I am reading and rereading *The Tiger in the Grass,* an exquisite collection of short stories and essays, written when she was eighty-five and her son was dying. In it, I find the piece on memory and commit it to *my* memory, to take out on days when I wonder if I will be in my seventies or eighties when the words I write will be cherished and committed to memory by readers just like me.

Years ago, I read a book by Tillie Olsen called *Silences,* in which Olsen asserted that so many fine and good and worthwhile women writers can create only when the years of doing and tending to others are ended. Not just homemakers, of course, but all those women who work two jobs to raise children alone, or are helpmeet or muse to a creative or powerful man, and so do not find the time or space or inner or outer permission to develop until they are much older. Who, in fact, sometimes never create the time or space in which to develop a body of work. They are not the recipients of grants or fellowships. They are invisible. The silence of these lost women is, in Tillie Olsen's mind, a travesty.

I remember watching a dramatization of one of Tillie Olsen's short stories on PBS one evening. It was the much-quoted piece "I Stand Here Ironing," a blue-collar woman's monologue, set in a rundown apartment, with a protagonist who encapsulates, in the ironing, all of her life and what she has done for others. And who still stands. Who still goes on. Who still reflects on life. Who still has something of value to say to others.

The world-renowned poet and essayist Maya Angelou is in her seventies. Toni Morrison, the National Book Award and Nobel Prize winner and the recipient of a MacArthur grant, is in her sixties and enjoying a renaissance of her writings. The poet and novelist May Sarton was still writing in her eighties and being published up to her death.

My favorite spiritual writer of the twentieth century is not Thomas Merton or C. S. Lewis or Joseph Campbell. It is Madeleine L'Engle, certainly the finest and most prolific of the American Christian writers of this century. She is, according to a manuscript by her I recently reviewed, now eighty years old, while her cowriter, Lucy Shaw, a fine poet in her own right, is in her mid-sixties.

We have so much to say. A younger male editor asked me once how much research I had to do while writing a novel about four generations of women growing up in an old Victorian house in Texas during World War II. "None," I answered him, startled. "I lived it."

We have lived it all, from turn-of-the-century reminiscences handed down from our foremothers, to tales of the Great Depression and two World Wars, recollected from our own memories.

We have so much to say. Harriet Doerr wrote her evocative lines while recalling all the houses she had ever lived in, in more than eighty years, including her years in Mexico, where a campesino once described to her the phenomenon of sleeves of water raining down on parched and arid land, while close by other fields were left dry.

There may have been times when years and years of living with others and for others took precedence over the creative spark within, when nurturing meant a sick child or a fractious husband or an aging relative, rather than meaning the nursing, the nurturance, of the work within us. Yet a dream deferred is not a dream denied. There is still time.

We have been silent far too long. No more excuses. No "It's too late" or "My life is over" or "No one wants to hear me." It's our turn.

Today is a day of receiving. No more parched landscapes. No more arid wastes. No more silences. Just this, with purpose and with gratitude. To know that you have everything you need. As do I. "A square of sky, a piece of stone, a page, a pen, and memory raining down on me in sleeves."

READING MYSTERIES

I read constantly. If I don't have a good book, I'm beside myself.

GAIL GODWIN

$\mathcal{I}$ like to read mystery novels. Why? Especially since I am not overly fond of blood and gore, horror, violence, or victims of violent crime. I read mystery stories for the same reason I read Nancy Drew, Girl Detective, when I was growing up. Mystery stories present a heroine or hero engaged in solving a puzzle. Mysteries do have dead bodies, unfortunately. They also have crisis, cool-headed logic, and sometimes but not always, compassion. They often also contain wit, irony, and humor, three of my favorite things. Most contain a large dose of competence, a little danger, and a thoroughly satisfactory ending. In mysteries, the good are rewarded while the evil are punished. In mysteries, the world regains order after upset. In mysteries, evil can be solved.

The witty, ironic, intrepid protagonists of modern mystery fiction (like Kinsey Millhone, Sue Grafton's series P.I.) are independent and gutsy to the core. They (usually, but not always, women investigators) cut right through layers of bureaucracy and social lies, evasions and justifications, in order to bring the bad guys to justice, all the while commenting on the lies we tell ourselves and others in order to justify less than noble behavior. I like that.

I like the classic British mysteries the best. Very little blood and guts. No pornography, and except for the hapless corpse, which serves as the focal point for the puzzle, very little violence. Everyone is so stiff-upper-lipped. Only the reader is privy to the seething, complex psychological depths of P. D. James's Chief Inspector Adam Dalgliesh. Only the reader is aware and chuckling gleefully as Agatha Christie's Miss Marple is underestimated and dismissed by both the authorities and the local murderer. Yet by the end of the tale she will solve the murder, like a genteel wise crone, putting everything back to rights, tidily, all in place.

Perhaps you are not familiar with the characters I mention. No matter. Although you will be well served to make their acquaintance. There! That sounds suitably English mystery phrasing. No matter.

Because these characters are mythic archetypes. Something within each of us resonates and responds to their heroic ingenuity. They are like us as we would wish to be in moments of crisis. They put the world to rights.

I wish life were more like a mystery novel. I'd like to be both courageous and competent, clear-headed and compassionate. I'd like to bring the bad guys down. City streets would be safer, politics would be more idealistic, there would be neighbors instead of gangs, no child would suffer pain or poverty, and most of all, good would *always* win.

DREAMING THE SELF

*The dry twigs left of a vanished life, whatever its
fullness once was, are rubbed together until they
catch fire.*

PATRICIA HAMPL

$\mathcal{O}$nce upon a time, I was married for many more years than I wanted, to a man who hated women. He had many good qualities—I searched high and low to find them—but his essential character drove me to solitude, lest I become as rigid and mean-spirited as he. I yearned for freedom, while I did all the right things and more, sacrificing my nature to unrequited, unnoticed, unfulfilled love.

I wrote a poem when I was in my forties, called "Dreaming the Self." It was years more before I left him. I could not, at that place and space in time, see my way clear past closed doors and boxed-in rooms and a life made of pretending and niceness.

Eventually I fled my old life and came to the ocean, where I learned harsh, liberating lessons, while I became myself.

Here is the poem.

DREAMING THE SELF

I have seen dreams in back of other
women's eyes,
A certain filming over, a certain knowing,
There, next to the eyelids' creases.

I wonder what they do with their sly secrets,
As they plow onward, plant, plan, thrive
In busy, rigid gardens?
They survive.
They do not break in pieces.

But I know one who seized the dream,
Who fled the reaping and the sowing.
I wonder if she lives?

She who was once as beautiful, as young as you,
I wonder if it all came true?
I wonder when this dream of being ceases.

Ten years later, I wrote to myself:

Now I have fled the past, and in the fleeing,
Now I have come full circle into seeing,
Now I have come from dreaming into being.

And knew the end of the poem.

MISS EULALIA DANCING

If you approach each new person you meet in a spirit of adventure, you will find yourself endlessly fascinated by the new channels of thought and experience and personality that you encounter. I do not mean simply the famous people of the world, but people from every walk and condition of life.

ELEANOR ROOSEVELT

$\mathcal{I}$ walk most mornings, weather permitting, within a beautiful labyrinth of spacious Victorian homes set back from parkland and cleared brush that overlooks the city proper from a high bluff. I've gotten my best ideas from these walks, from the rhythm of my sneakers that translates into rhythmic sentences. I've written my last six books this way, encountering synchronicity and stories at every bend in the road.

This summer, walking just after dawn, I rounded a corner and saw, on the green, cleared parkland across from the imposing houses, an amazing sight. I saw an elderly woman dancing barefoot in the grass. She was tall and thin and fluttery and graceful. She was dressed in a calf-length, gauzy, free-floating cotton dress with red flowers and green and yellow leaves on a black background. Her sandals lay in the street. An old Cadillac sedan was parked next to the curb.

I stopped in my tracks. She continued dancing, her arms swooping like fluttery birds, her eyes half-closed, her strong, ugly, gnarled feet lifting lightly on the grass. She saw me. She hesitated, almost stopped, then caught herself from falling. She waved at me, lifted her arms again, and continued dancing.

I went on my way, bemused. I thought up an entire life for her. I named her Miss Eulalia. I thought of her as a slightly loony spinster aunt, like the ones in southern gothic novels who are kept in attics. How had she escaped? And if she was "slightly off," as my grandmother would say, how then could she dance with such joy, such abandon? I put the image away for another day. I did not encounter her again on subsequent mornings, although I looked for her footprints in the grass. Maybe she was a figment of my overactive imagination. Maybe it was I who longed to dance at dawn.

About ten days later I took a late-afternoon walk instead of my usual early-morning one. On a doubled-back street in the circle of homes, about a mile along my walk, in front of an imposing, three-storey granite structure, I saw the Cadillac. It was parked in the driveway, and I had to detour around it on the sidewalk in order to get by. Its doors flew open and lo and behold, Miss Eulalia emerged, clutching grocery bags, a dry cleaner's bag slung over one arm. She was dressed—I swear it's true!—in the same fluttering, bright, gauzy dress that she had worn in her dawn dancing. This time her sandals were firmly on her feet. She smiled at me and said good afternoon, the way southerners do when they encounter passing strangers, and I smiled in return. Her face was full of wrinkles and she was even skinnier than I thought.

"Hello!" I said back. "I thought it was you." Her grocery bags threatened to fall out of her arms. I caught one before it toppled to the sidewalk.

"Oh, oh, oh!" she said in a high, breathless voice. "You saw me!"

The front door opened behind her. A woman in a white uniform, wheeling an ancient woman in a wheelchair, stood silhouetted in the doorway.

Miss Eulalia put a conspiratorial finger to her lips. "Don't tell!" she whispered.

The woman in the wheelchair called to her. "Coming, Mother," Miss Eulalia said. She reached out to me for the grocery bag. "I used to be a teacher," she confided in that same fluttery, high-pitched voice, smiling all the while. "But after retirement, and Mother needed me, and I'm the only daughter," her voice trailed off to a whisper. "You know how it is."

"I used to be a teacher too," I said to her. She turned to go, distracted, her arms full of chores. "What did you teach?" I asked her. I wanted her to stay. I wanted to know who she was and how she continued her life and why she danced at dawn, and why it had to be a secret.

"Music," she said. "I taught music." She turned to go into the house. She hefted the waiting bags into the uniformed woman's arms. I walked on.

"Wait!" she said. She danced after me. "Maybe I'll see you in the park again," she said. "When I can get away. It's my amusement. It's my music. But don't tell!" she pleaded. "Don't ever tell."

Another querulous, preemptory call from the woman in the wheelchair and she was gone.

I walk by the cleared land on the edge of the bluff again and again. Now the grass is bare and turning yellow in the summer drought. It is empty. There are no footprints in the grass, no discarded sandals, no fluttery figure swooping and bending in a private, ecstatic dance.

Questions dance through me as well. What does she do now to escape from imposed expectations? Why can't she, and did she ever, dance and make music in her tower room? Where does her duty lie? What has happened to Miss Eulalia, who once taught music? who made her own music?

How I hope that, somewhere, Miss Eulalia is alive and well and free. How I hope that Miss Eulalia is dancing.

I TOLD YOU SO

The old woman I shall become will be quite different from the woman I am now. Another I is beginning.

*M*y son who works in publishing sends me a book he is enthusiastic about. "It's about true women," he says excitedly. "Brave, strong, sturdy, hardy women. It's sweeping the publishing community by storm. And Mom, there's another book. It's about mature love, about old people loving and losing, but remembering their love for always, and it's on the best-seller list."

"Old people?"

"Well, you know, in their fifties. It's a whole new trend."

In their fifties? What about their sixties? Their seventies? I could have told him about mature love. If he had asked.

Three prominent women have written books discovering menopause. I've already been there. I remember Margaret Mead asserting, "There is no power on earth like the zest of the postmenopausal woman." In ten years, the three prominent women will know this.

I could have told them so.

A friend tells me of a magnificent book that taps into the

wild and primitive and instinctual nature of women. She is a conventional, traditional, professional woman, married to a very old man. She supports them both, although he controls the purse strings.

"I'm going to get it," she says excitedly. "No telling where this may lead."

I could have told her.

Once before my mother became ill she came over to my house and commented on the books on my shelves that tell of women's natures, women's wounds, women's strengths, women's power.

"How did I ever have a child like you?" she said, half-laughing, more than a little puzzled, a little scared. She has no idea.

I could have told her.

In ministry, in medicine, in business, in literature, and in politics, women come forth that have labored for years in the vineyard shadows. They cannot be ignored. They cannot be dismissed. They cannot be stuffed back into their boxes. Women come forth in their nature and in their nurture, in their power and in their politics. Women come forth in their creativity and in their wisdom.

These magnificent women from fifty to eighty are our most underrated, undervalued resource. Such a woman is a natural mentor for younger women. She can show the way through the tribulations and the triumphs of love, loss, birth, death, illness, aging, caregiving, and renewal. This woman may have forged an individual and courageous life of creativity and solitude. Or survived divorce or widowhood, only to come into that sweet sense of self that welcomes either sex or celibacy, knowing that she is whole and complete in herself. Whether teacher or secretary, homemaker or CEO, family caregiver or professional therapist, the value of the mature woman is deep, rich, enduring, dynamic, powerful, courageous, and wise. She is the well of wisdom for us all. She is the scout that goes forth into uncharted territory and reports back to the rest of us. This is what I have learned. This is what I have created for myself. My own way may be different from yours, but there are life lessons along the way that I will share with you. We will both be enriched by this sharing.

In an unpublished novel I once wrote called *Families,* I had the main character, a mature woman, say to the reader near the end of the tale: "Now I am more than word-weaver, tale-receiver. I am the story itself. I am the wise woman, come to complete the circle."

We are all wise women, those of us of a certain age who have so much to give. We are all teachers, mentors, caregivers, way-showers for each other. We complete the circle.

I could have told you so.

GOOD OL' BOYS AND GOOD OL' GIRLS

Reading is a private, intimate act for which we are accountable to no one.

SHIRLEY HAZZARD

*O*nce upon a time, when I lived with my family in a house filled with books, a good ol' boy came over one night with a passel of other people for a meeting, and he paused, thunderstruck, on the threshold.

Now if you're not from Texas, maybe you're not quite sure what a good ol' boy is. You may have seen a caricature or two in car chase movies about the South, and concluded that a good ol' boy is someone who has less between his ears than on his belly, thinks he's God's gift to women, swaggers and spits and chaws (as in chawin' tobacco), loves his guns and his hunting dawgs, quit school early, sometimes works in a blue-collar or uniform job (I hear there are some in the Senate as well), and generally lives in the same county as his daddy afore him. A good ol' boy, while he has many fine qualities, gets stuck somewheres between 1945 and 1960, and doesn't allow as how anything has happened to change the world since then that he'd be interested in. There are a lot of good ol' boys where I come from.

This particular specimen, I'll call him a GOB for short, stopped dead in his tracks when he saw the walls of books lining the living room where we were meeting. He shook his head in bemusement. "I ain't never seen so many books at once," he said. "What do you use them for?"

This startled me. "Why, uh, to read, of course," I replied, feeling, like Alice, curiouser and curiouser.

"Naw," he said. "No kidding. You read *all* them books?"

"Well, most of them," I said.

"You ain't one of them libbers, are you?" he asked vehemently.

I was not sure I understood him. And then I did.

"I guess so," I said neutrally. Darn if I was going to be apologetic in my own home.

"Naw," he said again. "Can't be."

"Yes," I replied, " 'fraid so."

He took off his cowboy hat and scratched his head. I noticed his face was red from sun and beer while his hair was white and thinning. I began to feel sorry for him. Live and let live and all that.

Then he worked his chaw over to the other side of his jaw, looked around covertly for a jar or a vase or something that could be used as a spittoon, and delivered the final insult.

"Well, what I wants to know then, is this: If you read all them books, when do you have time to be a woman?"

I had no answer for him. I couldn't even compute the question.

Years later, I am sitting in a restaurant with several of my women friends. We are all in our fifties and sixties, well-educated professional women who number, among our respective credentials, an artist, a writer, a legal mediator, a business-woman, a social worker, and a school counselor. We are all shapes and sizes and colors and backgrounds, but we have one thing in common that I am struck by. We are all Texas women, born and bred. We all grew up in small towns with good ol' boys in the background, as fathers or brothers or husbands or employers or employees. We grew up as good little girls, some of us in the midst of the Depression, some of us in the postwar years, one of us in the barrio, one with handicapped parents. Surrounded by good ol' boys at every turn.

And this is what we did. We educated ourselves, supported our husbands, and in some cases, discarded them. We raised our children. We work in the world, in whatever ways our talents and our inclinations lead us. We serve. We all grew up working poor, and now we are comfortable. Comfortable in our skins. Comfortable in who we are.

I wonder sometimes how we survived the good ol' boy syndrome, and our own "good little girl" syndrome, to become what we are now. I wonder if anyone, looking at us, would call us "good ol' girls."

I propose a toast. "Here's to the good ol' girls," I cry, and we drink to that, laughing.

I wonder how we ever, surrounded as we were on all sides and for so many years by good ol' boys, became the women that we are.

Maybe it was all the books.

NOTHING IS EVER WASTED

The good thing about becoming older is that you gain time from that much more experience and can see where the real stories are.

GAIL GODWIN

I'm sorting through old manuscripts today. Reams of paper, some scrawled longhand, some old carbons from the time before word processors. Hundreds of poems. Thousands of pages. Some published. Most not. Sorting. What to keep? What to discard?

This is my life. Reconstructed through words on paper. I can count decades by the paper artifacts that mark my passage.

I'm startled by my poetry. Did I really have those insights, that command of language, that flash of fire? I was so young. What did I know of the real world? Correction—outer world. I see now that I knew far more than I ever admitted of that inner world of light and magic where words string together to hum in your head, and only after you've written a poem do you discern its meaning. There are poems here that tell me more of who I am than they did when the words came sizzling and churning through my brain, through my breastbone, through my fingers, until at last they subsided into patterns of black lines on white paper.

Here are the wonder years. Here are the learning years. Here are the bitter years. Here are the joyful years. Here are the weary years. Here are the lost years, blank pages never written on, nothing recorded, nothing of me left to be recorded. Here am I.

Use it! Use it or lose it! Use everything you were, everything you are. Use grief and rage. Use words to move you forward. Use joy, too, if you can ever, ever find it.

A friend told me that first you learn through pain. Then, if you are very lucky and very wise, you learn to learn through joy. That's if and when you can take your pain and transform it somehow, by whatever alchemy exists within your blood and bones, transmute it into a gentle joy that comes when you least expect it, that comes when you have emptied out the pain, and a vacuum rushes in, and the joy flows forward, like the rage and the fear once did. Come now to a place of joy.

I wove my soul into these poems. Here are all the seasons of a woman's life. Here are the words that speak of "perilous poetry." There are the words that speak of abstinence—"The spirit is not willing, the flesh is not weak." Here are transcendent shining holy moments caught and held—"There was the stretching of arms out to embrace / All of the clean clear thereness of space, / And she knew at least for a moment where she was." I even found a poem that I wrote when I was fierce about the loss of the young and hopeful woman within me. Now, and only now, so many years later, do I see its joy. Now, only years later, can I chant its curve of syllables and

feel the power and the truth within them as I told my lost su-
perwoman, "Nothing is ever wasted, merely postponed."

And so it is, on this rainy day, sorting through the debris
of my emotions, sorting through passions, intensities, longings, love lost and love regained. Fly forward. Work forward.
Use it all. Hold the pages in your hands and let them flutter
through to make a treasure on the pine wood floors. Regret
nothing! Use it all! This is your work. It is of value. It matters.
You are a writer. Record it. Care for it. Rejoice. Nothing is
ever wasted. Merely postponed.

IF YOU WANT TO BE A WRITER

The greatest gift is the passion for reading. It is cheap, it consoles, it distracts, it excites, it gives you knowledge of the world and experience of a wide kind. It is a moral illumination.

ELIZABETH HARDWICK

When I was eight years old, you could travel the whole city where I grew up, safely and alone, children and adults alike. So when I was eight years old, I was issued a library card and allowed to take the bus at the corner and go downtown to Eighth and Throckmorton and bring books home to read. Every week. The limit was ten books. I took it to the limit. Mr. Carnegie had—bless his soul and thank you very much!—built an imposing granite and limestone edifice, several stories high, that jutted out from its corner location like the brow of a massive ship. My library card was my passport. The books were my adventures.

I read in the porch swing in the summertime, with a pillow behind my head to cushion the wooden slats, rocking myself occasionally with a push of my bare feet so that the swing itself, and I in it, could rhythm to the sound of the words, all those beautiful, magical words that transported me far, far away from Fort Worth, Texas, in the middle of the Second World War. In the wintertime I would read in an attic alcove, where my cousins and my sister and I slept. They slept. I didn't. I read by flashlight, I read from the light of the lamppost, I read by the moon and the light of the stars.

Once a reader, always a reader. I taught my children that, and we all read, in bed and out, everything we have time for and can get our hands on. Books are still magical adventures that transport us out of our ordinary, mundane, everyday world.

When I was living in L.A., I went to hear Ray Bradbury speak. I had read his books and studied his style. I had *been* one of the "live books" that walked in the snow at the end of *Fahrenheit 451,* the living humans who held the stories in their heads while the books themselves did, indeed, burn at that precise degree of heat on which the title of the book was based.

What did he tell us, this white-haired mountain of a tale-teller? A woman in the front row asked the question we all wanted to ask. (It was not me.)

"To what," she asked in a precise, no-nonsense tone, "do you attribute your success as a writer?"

"Madam," he answered her courteously. Would no one ask about the creative process, the dream state, the flow of consciousness that wove the past into future worlds of fantasy and emotion? Success. All right. So be it.

"Madam," he said, his leonine head swiveling in her direction, his spectacles glinting on us all, so that we could not see his eyes. "I attribute my success to a habit I have had ever since I was eight years old. I make it my habit to go into a library or a bookstore every day—every day!—that is my success, that is why I am a writer."

"But why?" she persisted.

"Because, madam," he almost roared at her, "that is where the books are."

TOO MANY TEAKETTLES

If no one else gives me value, I give it to myself.

JO ANN LORDAHL

I am a woman with too many teakettles. I burn them up at a moment's notice, because of dreaming my way through a morning's composing, because of wrestling with a knotty paragraph, because of talking too long on the phone while a teakettle forgets to whistle and sputters, inevitably, to a charred stop.

A friend of mine who is a bodywork therapist tells me that most of her clients, especially women, think that they are either "too much" or "not enough." Too much woman, too much to handle, too exuberant, too passionate, too needy, greedy, demanding, emotional—you name it, we've been called it, from exhortations in long-ago childhoods from adults who longed to mold us into good little girls to insecure men who tell us that we are too much because they fear that they cannot tame us.

There's a lot of "not enough" going on around us and within us too. From downsizing to debt, from too little time to too little love, we women (some of us sometimes, and most of us at one time or another) are faced with "not enough."

Not enough of me to go around, not enough of me to learn, do, be. Not enough energy, not enough love. How can we ever get our lives right when we are either too much or not enough?

My friend the fantastic bodyworker counsels balance. She counsels alignment and attention as well. Paying attention to what we say to our bodies, so that we can change the messages we are giving forth of too much or not enough. Counseling attention to the messages our bodies are trying to teach us with every breath and every excess pound and every unresolved, long-held pain. Listening. Seesawing our way into a balance point. Making corrections as we go along, until we can say to ourselves, "You are not too much or too little. You are just right."

What does this have to do with too many teakettles? I figured it out. I seldom buy things for myself. I learned frugality at an early age. I'm not a shopper, not a great consumer, except maybe of books and ideas. But whenever the ten-dollar or twenty-dollar teakettle blows its stack (metaphorically) and burns up with the speed of light, so that before I can get to the stove it is ruined beyond repair and must be replaced immediately, well, then, I get a treat, don't I? I get to go out on a sunny afternoon (after I've finished my work, of course) and find myself the prettiest, shiniest teakettle I can. I get to start over with the new, and since (except for water) tea is the only beverage I drink, nurture my addiction as well. And all for ten to twenty dollars for a have-to-have item.

What do *you* do when you feel that you are not enough or,

conversely, too much? Crying jag? Unwise love affair? Shopping spree? Chocolate? As my wise friend says to me as she gently massages my neck, "Pay attention." Even when your solution to a temporary lack of balance is buying and burning too many teakettles.

WRITING MAGIC

Creativity is really the structuring of magic.

ANNE KENT RUSH

$\mathcal{W}$riters use magic all the time. We use our dreams, our visions, our experiences, our deep heart's longing, to create from out of the clear blue and then down and through the brain, the mind, the eyes, the hands, onto paper, typewriter, or computer screen, the magic. There's nothing else to call it, when you come right down to it. Then we revise our dreams and stories, let the printer hum their crisp symbols onto blank pages churning the filled pages out onto the desk. Then we bundle up our dreams and stories, our own myths made manifest, and send them out into the world. Then, if we are lucky, wise, brave, and talented, we sell our magic.

And our dreams and myths and magic are then translated outward into a beautiful, enduring book, which goes on bookstore shelves everywhere.

Then and only then, if we are lucky, wise, brave, and talented, a reader will come into the bookstore and breathe in the smell and the feel of all those books, breathe in the stories and the myths and the magic of all those thousands of books that cry out to be read. She will search among the shelves and drum her fingers along the bright bindings and take out one or two or three and study the covers, which promise magic, myths, and story-telling, and flip through the pages, and with a sigh, put one or two or three back.

And then if we are very, very lucky, a book will fall out of its high shelf into her hands, like a gift, like a sign, like a portent, omen, promise, and she will take that book and pay for it and bring it home. Then she will sit in her easy chair, when the day's work is done, and open the book and engage herself in the pages of black symbols on white paper. The fire will die down and the cat will want to be let out, and the phone will ring, and it is far, far past her bedtime, yet she reads on. Every page. Every last blessed page.

Then she will clasp the book to her heart and cry out, "Yes, yes. That's the way it is." Or she will shake her head, thoughtful, bemused, and flip back to a page or two, to see if she has understood. Or maybe she will read the book again, more slowly, turning down the corners of the pages, making marks in the margins, adding her thoughts and emotions to the ones already printed on the page. Maybe she will tell her friends.

And then, and then! Maybe, just maybe, if we are very, very, very lucky, brave, wise, and talented, she will change her life.

V

Spirit Strengthened

Caregiving,
Courage,
Power,
and Prayer

SPIRIT STRENGTHENED

*The especial genius of women I believe to be electrical
in movement, intuitive in function, spiritual in tendency.*

MARGARET FULLER

I believe this too. I believe that as we grow older, wiser, more loving, more tuned in to Spirit, that Spirit connects with us and helps us to be whole. We are Spirit strengthened for the rest of our journey.

It does not matter by what name you call this force of Spirit. You may call it God, Jesus Christ, Buddha, Krishna, Allah, angels and archangels, the Holy Spirit, the feminine face of God, or a universal force for good. You have your own deep faith. I will not question it or try to change it.

Metaphysicians often talk of God in everyday life as Good Orderly Direction. This is what Julia Cameron calls it. She says: "When the word *God* is used . . . you may substitute the thought *Good Orderly Direction* or *Flow.* What we are talking about is a creative energy. . . . The point is not what you name it. The point is that you try using it. For many of us, thinking about it as a form of spiritual electricity has been a very useful jumping-off place."

Oh what fantastic and evocative words! To think of creative energy as spiritual electricity. To think of the energy of God as spiritual electricity. And sometimes, when the still, small voice calls to you, to think of yourself as a woman who is made of electricity. The electricity that fuels and heals your blessed body. The electricity that rearranges thought so that you are clearer and freer in your thinking and can access your radiant mind. The electricity that bursts old emotional patterns, dissolving old mistakes and jettisoning bitter baggage, so that you can call upon your passionate emotions to lead you to joy and wholeness. And the spiritual electricity that fuels your inner self, so that your trust deepens and your strength widens to encompass all that you bring to your mature and abundant life.

Sometimes you may feel anything but energetic, much less electrical, in nature or creativity, as your spirit strengthens through difficult circumstances. We all have losses in life. In these next pages you will find others who can share with you the dark journeys as well as the shining summit. There's joy too, though, along the way to enlightenment. There's love as well as duty. There's power, too, as you take your own life into your own heart and hands, and make of it, despite the dark times, a sustaining and renewing resource.

You are Spirit Strengthened by both adversity and awe, by both pain and power. Claim Spirit as well as Body Blessed, Mind Radiant, Emotions Passionate. Claim all as one, integrated into daily tasks and increased wisdom year by year. You are a woman of Spirit. Rejoice and be thankful.

MASTERING DUTY

I do not want the peace which passeth understanding,
I want the understanding which bringeth peace.

HELEN KELLER

$\mathcal{W}$hen I lived in L.A. for seven intense and fateful years, I had a chance to explore an astonishing arrray of mind/body/spirit disciplines, some absurd, most helpful, all revealing. I could give you a dazzling laundry list of personal development therapies and theories, but unless you've been there, done that, it wouldn't mean much. I've never been self-indulgent, just curious. And I needed to find new ways of healing and restoring myself after great tragedy.

One of the ways I did this was with my dream exploration. Another was through meditation. Yet another was through past-life regression. And in every one of my explorations, a woman, a stranger, would come to me. She was dressed all in black, with long skirts, high-topped shoes, a set of keys dangling at her waist. She wore a cowl and a medieval cross. She was commanding, regal, decisive, ascetic. Her soul burned through her sharp blue eyes. She was the busiest woman I have ever seen. Pacing through stone corridors, sitting at judicial hearings, supervising grounds and fields and harvests, feeding the sick, ministering to the poor, perusing documents and illuminated manuscripts, writing letters in an elegant hand, singing in choir, baptizing the young and burying the dead. I called her the Great Administrator, for want of a better name, although she later revealed to me that she was "the Mother Abbess known as Dame Elizabeth." Although I am not a Catholic, I recognized her as an archetype from the past, someone's past—mine?—and finally settled on the strength that she could give me rather than questioning the source of this recurring vision.

You must realize that I wasn't sitting around communing with the spirits during the years that Dame Elizabeth appeared to me. I was running a company, writing and publishing and traveling and lecturing and coping concurrently with the death of my son (and other people I loved) and a lingering chronic illness. When I was very tired, Dame Elizabeth would come to me in my dreams. She was indomitable and focused and wise and sure, qualities I longed for and felt lacking in me.

When I moved back to Texas seven years later, Dame Elizabeth disappeared. Until, that is, a gentle, wise counselor started a group that explored past lives. This is how she explained the process to the group. "It doesn't matter if you believe in past lives and reincarnation or not. It doesn't matter if you have read the books and studied the theories. You don't have to give up your own belief system or your religious upbringing. This is just a tool, in order for you to explore ways in which your unconscious can be of help to you while solving problems. It's okay if you feel that you are just 'making it up?' What is important is that you are open to receiving insights that can help you now."

After a self-awareness process that led into a relaxed state, the six of us in the small group began to explore the images that flashed across our closed eyes and open minds. These images turned into stories, complete with time, place, physical sensations, emotional depth, conflict and resolution.

Well of course you know what happened next. Dame Elizabeth appeared in all her great administrative glory. Tirelessly and faithfully, she fulfilled her duties, with an occasional side look at me from out of her penetrating eyes. Year after year I followed her progress through the cloister walls. I saw her adjudicating disputes. I saw her baking bread. I saw her anguish in her private prayers. I saw her steely resolve. She lived her faith.

I heard the voice of the counselor through my reverie. "Move forward to the time of death of the life image you are experiencing," she said softly. "Go through the closure of this person's life, and ask this person to give you a gift. A gift can be a symbol, a gesture, some words of wisdom to help you in your own present life. What does this image want to tell you? Listen well."

Dame Elizabeth was very old when she laid down her ring of keys. Her long, slender, blue-veined hands crossed over her breasts, she lay in peaceful repose as masses were sung for her. She was released in ceremony after a long and useful life. I could hear her thoughts clearly as the music and the ritual bore her home. "I wish I had loved more and mastered duty less."

Her words echoed to the very core of me. "I wish I had loved more and mastered duty less."

Thank you for the gift, Dame Elizabeth. I will heed it well. Thank you for your strength and wisdom and faith. Thank you for your spiritual dedication and your administrative skills. In all the years that you have lent me your strength and your example, I never knew until now of your greatest gift to me.

"I wish I had loved more and mastered duty less." So do I, dear inner helper, dear divine teacher, dear holy feminine archetype. So do I.

PRIVATE FAITH AND PUBLIC PRAYER

It is not until you come to a spiritual understanding of who you are—not necessarily a religious feeling, but deep down, the spirit within—that you can begin to take control.

OPRAH WINFREY

$\mathcal{W}$hen I visit churches, hospice groups, and women's retreat groups in the course of my work, I am struck by the underlying unity among the various and disparate expressions of faith that I enounter. Whether Episcopal or Methodist or Presbyterian or Baptist or Lutheran or Congregational, whether Unity or Religious Science, whether something as different as a metropolitan community church with a membership mostly of gays and lesbians, or a Roman Catholic AIDS retreat, everyone (or so it seems to me) is going back to God. Some of us never went away.

I like to be a good guest when I visit differing faiths. To show respect for belief systems that may be different from mine. To learn from a Buddhist meditation retreat or from a bar mitzvah, and come away stronger, uplifted, and more reflective. I don't think that being ecumenical waters down my faith. It is a personal and private one, and it draws on transcendental silence and long private rounds of prayer, more than the ritual in the Episcopal church I grew up in. Although I love the ritual still, I love my private communion best.

Many women as they grow older find that church or temple gives to them the solace and the continuity of community that they seek. The churches I visit are full of devout and committed women who put their faith tirelessly into action.

I do have trouble with two things. One is loud, overt public prayer (Pharisees, anyone?). In the buckle of the Bible belt in which I live, you are not asked what you do for a living. You are asked, first and foremost, "What is your church affiliation?" Then you are often labeled based on that one query.

A woman hospice chaplain once spoke to me about how the work she has done with the dying has changed her. "I no longer believe in a patriarchal, theist God," she told me. "But I do believe in God." We shared with one another a little of our work over the years and concluded that the women and men we knew who worked in this field used spiritual action as their expression of the God-force within. The old "Faith without works is dead" principle.

I draw the line at condemning others for not believing and practicing as I do. My life and the way that I live it is between me and my God. It's really none of your business. I'm uneasy, too, at the fervent public prayers that seek to change God's mind or mine. I feel uncomfortable praying aloud at a restaurant or other social gathering, as some of my more zealous friends and relatives insist. But I will say grace and mean it at a private function. It is also common, in the part of the country where I live, for other people to say to me "I'll pray for you" and mean it most sincerely. But what if their prayers are manipulative and cajoling? What if their prayers are more about telling God, Jesus Christ, or the Holy Spirit what they think God should do for my own good and theirs, instead of asking for and allowing a Divine outcome? No thanks, I'm no spiritual dictator.

When I am left alone to develop my own contemplative spiritual life I am peaceful. At the very least, I learn my own spiritual lessons, instead of having other people's opinions thrust upon me. I can then look at myself and others as having a spark of the Divine within each one, all the while knowing that to my humble knowing at this point in time, there is also a Divine force for Good in the universe, by whatever name or denomination you may call it.

One of my friends is a practicing Buddhist, and has found great serenity in the "Four-Fold Truths" and the "Eight-Fold Path." One of my friends, born Jewish, studies both the Kabbalah and the Course in Miracles, with increasing delight. I write for several inspirational and denominational publications, including *Unity* and *Science of Mind,* and find great joy in the perennial and nonjudgmental philosophy they espouse.

One of our tasks as mature women, it seems to me, is to separate the wheat from the chaff and find the set of spiritual principles and spiritual truths by which we intend to live for the rest of our lives. This has very little to do with religion and quite a lot to do with our own intuitive connection to the Divine. Not all of us are mystics. But none of us are sheep either. The faith of our fathers may serve us still, with a larger vision. Or we may break with tradition and find our own way, unencumbered by what we are supposed to think. The search itself is a holy one. And along the way we will, as women have from time immemorial, put our faith into action. Just like my friend the hospice chaplain. That well may be the greatest blessing of all.

SOLIDITY OR FLAME?

When we see the core of our being as full, we are like the constantly radiating sun. We have plenty to give and share.

PATRICIA REMELE

$\mathcal{I}$n the meditation that I pour myself into daily, there is a portion of that prayer time in which you move your consciousness from the head into the heart and contemplate the altar of God within you, there at your heart center, there at the core of your being.

For months I struggled with this concept, for I could feel and sense no stone altar, no imposing edifice, nothing to worship to, nothing to worship from. What I found instead was a sense of warmth growing within me, until at the very thought of moving the energy of my head into the energy of my heart, the warmth became a candle. The candle lit, flickered, stayed firm. The candle rested within a white flower. The flower rested on deep blue water. The candle and the flower and the water contained, within me and my heart's core, that steady flame.

When I am sad or exhausted I call upon that image. Often all I have to do is close my eyes and put my hand over my breastbone, there in the center of my being, there where the sacred core of me resides.

This is not a new image by any means. How many philosophers and theologians and magical, mysterious avatars have talked about the fire of God? I know that it is not a new image. But it is *my* image.

Recently I ran across poems I had written years ago, when my life was so different that I could not recognize myself if I found myself in that landscape again. I was teaching immigrants at night then, and going to college in the daytime, and working a second job on the weekend, and raising four sons as a single parent. It was a time of great intensity and energy, a time in which you had to be young and strong and focused in order to survive, much less follow your dream. I was determined beyond belief. I was a veritable motion machine, juggling tasks and jobs and people like a magician. All my energy was focused outward, into the future. Surely I wasn't writing poetry then? There couldn't have been time.

But I found a series of poems I had written about my night-school students. They worked menial jobs all day long, they raised families in an unfamiliar land, and they came to school four nights a week to learn English, to get ahead, to find a place within the American landscape and language for their dreams to flourish. They were solid, dependable, focused. They were survivors, just like me.

One young girl, she must have been about ten, acted as translator for her parents and did her own English homework in the back of the room. She was beautiful, with dark, liquid eyes and a quick, agile way with words. She mothered her parents, even while she smoldered with intensity. Her name was Mary María. María was the name she had been given at birth in Mexico, and Mary was the name her parents added when they came to this country and she started school. So she was called Mary María and the name stuck, like two cultures entwined in one small body.

The poem I wrote about her asked the question, "Who will you become?" It said in part, "To be a poet and astound the world? / Or lean to safety, learn the narrow glance? / Who triumphs here, solidity or flame?"

That was, of course, my own question, my own quest. Who triumphs here, solidity or flame? I yearned to write. I yearned to astound the world and myself with the power contained within words. The power of words to teach, to inspire, to change a life. The power of words to burst into flame on the page.

Even then, the candle in the flower on the deep blue water must have been there in my heart. I yearned to follow my heart's passion. I thought I had to choose. Outwardly directed, or inwardly alive? Work of the world, or work of the soul? Earth or fire?

Now I can put my hand on my heart center and I can be both. I can be rooted, grounded, purposeful, and at the next moment—moving my focus upward, I can connect with the fire of my being. I can be flame. I can be a lighted candle, suspended in a white flower, sailing across the deep blue sea of my inner self. From that vantage point, I can see the fire within the heart of everyone I meet. Each one a Mary María, each one a clash of contradictions, each one a universe of longing.

I can see the candle in your own heart flickering and then steadying, firm, as you read these words. Who triumphs here, solidity or flame?

Choose both: to be grounded in earth, replenished by flame. Choose both. Then let your own light shine. Oh let it shine!

ALONG THE WAY TO
ENLIGHTENMENT

> *The excursion is the same when you go looking for your
> sorrow as when you go looking for your joy.*
>
> EUDORA WELTY

*M*y youngest son sent me a sweatshirt that said: "On your
way to enlightenment, bring snacks and a cookie." I laughed.

I'm writing this on my sixty-first birthday, a time to ponder not just where I've been but where I'm going and how
much time do I really have? For enlightenment? For wise, caring, creative living? For joy? And what should I bring along
with me on the journey?

I don't know if I've got forty years left to live, or thirty, or
twenty. What I do know, more and more as the days and the
years rush toward me, is that I want to spend the currency of
time and energy in ways that nourish my soul. So if you ask
me today what I will do with it, I will tell you that I have set
aside a time that refuses responsibility for a little while, that
turns aside, just for a day, from the virtuous self that pays
bills and gets the car inspected and washes dishes and evalu-
ates manuscripts and makes proactive phone calls that gener-
ate future income. I will tell the self that worries about the

future, especially about how to pay for it, to take a walk or a rest or a nap.

This essay was originally intended as a linear exercise in planning. For on our birthdays, just as on New Year's Day, don't most of us plan the year ahead? Making lists and adding up columns, griefs subtracted, blessings noted, unfulfilled aspirations written down for yet another year. I'm good at doing that. Putting my needs on paper so that they don't whirl fretfully around and around the inside of my head. Taking a deep breath and girding my loins for yet another year of trying, struggling, striving, keeping afloat, getting ahead. Will this work? Can I do this? And what if? Statistics on the poverty of older women, a visit to my mother in the nursing home, a newspaper report on cuts in social services—any and all of these things can initiate for me hours of feverish list-making, hours of measuring current resources against a sobering future. How much money will it take for me to get to future birthdays—as many birthdays as I want? You can get bogged down in future planning just as you can get bogged down in past rememberings.

Stop! I say to myself. And I mean it. How can I measure, why should I measure what the future holds? I have no way of knowing. No one can measure the dire and doom-filled moments that may lie just around the corner. Or the joy that may lie in wait for me as well.

What I can do, on this sweetly perfect spring day, is to take a notebook, a pen, an old chair, a favorite book, a sunshade, and spread my largesse out under a flowering tree. I can let my anxieties drop away like the drifts of white blossoms that fall around me. I can let the sun touch the closed lids of winter-weary eyes. I can breathe in the newness of now. And of course, along the way, along the daily journey to enlightenment, I can, will, do, must, bring snacks and a cookie.

The Deadliest Sin

All the arts we practice are apprenticeship. The big art is our life.

M. C. RICHARDS

$\mathcal{I}$ have three deadly sins I am continually trying to eradicate. They are anger, vanity, and self-pity. Seems as though the older you get, the more you ought to be able to not only recognize your weaknesses but root them out once and for all. Alas, I haven't got the knack of it yet!

My anger is quick, fast, soaring, awe-inspiring. It's a teakettle blowing up, popping and spitting and steaming and boiling. It subsides just as quickly, thank God, although its cousins, resentment and frustration, sometimes lurk in the bottom of the kettle for the rest of the day.

How do I handle these eruptions? Better than I used to. I used to think that you had to eradicate the weaknesses, the flaws, the errors, the mistakes, what I was taught as a child were called sins. What an old-fashioned word for negative emotions. What I was once told were "character defects."

Now that I've studied everything from conflict resolution to conscious breathing, from quantum physics to cognitive therapy, I've learned what transformation really entails. It is not annihilation. It's changing form. So anger can often serve as a spur to positive change. It can be a fire that lights us to reveal our passions for life. It can be a catalyst for change. And that's energy transformed from rage into action. It fuels you forward, instead of stopping you in your tracks. Anger harnessed to good can move mountains.

How about vanity? I no longer look in mirrors as I pass by, as I did when I was younger and full of myself. But, at the very least, vanity encourages me to present myself washed, dressed, groomed to face the world. Vanity compels me to eat right, exercise when I can, get enough sleep, keep my mind active and curious. Vanity and its cousin, pride, can create a job well done and a graceful way of interacting with the world.

You can have my self-pity. I've got enough for both of us and some left over for next week. It's been the bane of my emotional existence. Like an outraged housewife, I beat it out the back door with a broom whenever it rears its ugly head. I can tell myself that by feeling deeply I can learn compassion for others. Maybe. I can tell myself that passionate intensity fuels creative juices. Sometimes. I can tell myself that inner blame is better than outer blame. Not true. I can count my blessings, concoct an attitude of gratitude, do unto others instead of wallowing in whining. That helps. But not for long and not for always.

What I can do is to recognize the dark and bring it to the light. Face it, own it, ask for forgiveness of my self when it appears, ask for new perceptions, ask for release.

There is no age limit on eradicating weaknesses. And no guarantee that it can be done. Some roots lie deep. But once recognized, weaknesses can often be turned into strengths. I'm working on that premise for the deadliest sin of all.

In the meantime, do as I do. Grab a broom and sweep self-pity out the door. Be fierce. Be adamant. Be strong. Before it turns into a real character defect.

CAREGIVING AND COURAGE

From the moment I realized my mother would never again be the woman I knew, something fell inside of me. It did not fall with a crash, but was rather a slow, inexorable collapse. There was a strong green cord connecting me to this great, simple seeming, but complicated woman, who was herself rooted in the earth. I felt this cord weakening, becoming a thread. My legs seemed to be going out from under me. My heart felt waterlogged. My spirit lost its shine. My grief was kind enough to visit me only at night, in dreams: as I felt it wash over me, I did not care that I might drown. I knew that, awake, the unshed tears of rage and irremediable loss I was suffering would surely kill me. . . .

ALICE WALKER

Once when I was leading a discussion on caregiving at a local bookstore, a younger man in the audience began to tell of his own caregiving for his ailing mother, who had had a series of strokes. "I am only the secondary caregiver," he explained. "My father and the home health care nurse do most of the actual taking care. But I am there for her every night after work, and I am looking for ways to help and to connect with her. I am looking," he said somewhat desperately, "for something—anything—that can inspirit her—that can change her attitude, that can bring her happiness."

What he was really asking for, in great sincerity and love, was for things to be different. He explained that his mother was elderly, timid, a homemaker from a small-town background, and that now he wanted her to fight for her life, to live fully and consciously and aware, to do something—anything!—to fight the illness, the grief, the apathy, the depression that she had fallen into. "How can I inspirit her?" he kept asking.

"You can't," I told him. "Because you are not responsible for your mother's happiness." The words hit him like a blow. He swallowed and closed his eyes and blinked rapidly for a moment or two. "You cannot live her life for her. You cannot live her death for her. You cannot change her. You cannot change the experience she is going through. You can only show up. You can only show her your love, your unquestioning and accepting love, and hold her hand as she goes through her own experience."

He was, of course, asking for his own happiness as well. What can I do, what can I be, so that my mother will be changed, so that this situation can be changed, so that we can find some meaning in the face of long-term illness and unreasoning, incomprehensible debility? "How can my mother die?" he was asking.

I do not know the answer to this question which I too have pondered now for over six years and still counting, as my own dear, beloved mother dies inch by inch. I cannot save her, shield her, or make her happy. I cannot inspire her to live or inspire her to let go and die peacefully. It is her life. It is her journey. I am only the witness to the terrible and exhausting and ongoing struggle. I cannot bring her the gift of joy. I can only bring her my unwavering love.

"Inspirit," that odd and appropriate word the man used, comes, I believe, from the root word of "breath." To breathe the breath of life into someone. At least that is how I understood the man's question. Resuscitation.

Not all caregivers are women. But most of us are. Not all caregivers give up their jobs, jeopardize their own health, or exhaust their own lives in order to care for another, in order to inspirit another, in order to breathe life into the dying, in order to bring happiness to another. But most of us do. Most caregivers do attempt this impossible task. At some time or another most mature women, and a few men as well, become caregivers—primary caregiver or secondary caregiver or professional caregiver or everyday family caregiver. And it brings us to our knees. Every time. Whether we care for a child or an ailing parent, a spouse or a dear friend, a lover or a sibling. At some time we are brought to the questions "What can I do?" and "How shall I do it?" and "Show me the way to inspire and inspirit another person's life."

I have written books on caregiving. I have written books on death and dying and grief recovery and every aspect of the human soul, with all its struggles and all its questionings and all its longings. We teach what we most need to know. I write what I most need to know.

I am very, very tired of caregiving. I have done my part, I have walked the walk, I have paid my dues, I have gone through the dark night of the soul with more than one person that I loved dearly. I have let them go. There are no hauntings of unfinished business between me and the ones that I have loved, although there has been great sorrow at the circumstances.

There are few perfect deaths. Except for my maternal grandmother, who decided, on her seventy-ninth birthday, right after lunch, that she would sit down in her rocking chair in the summer sunlight and rest for just a moment. She died peacefully in that next moment, between the drawing in of one breath and the letting out of another, with a smile on her face and a hand on her heart. Except for that one instance, I can think of no one else I know who has gone gently into that good night or that good day. Except perhaps my son Michael. He was filled with a luminous will and a determination to spare, as best he could, the people that he loved just as he was determined to die consciously and courageously. In spirit. Inspiring us all. Between the drawing in of one breath and the letting out of another, he too was gone. There is nothing left now but the love.

That's what it really comes down to, doesn't it? That no matter the travail, no matter the shock, the exhaustion, the unanswered age-old questions, when we love and care wisely, when we just show up, again and again and again, there is nothing left but the love. The essence of the person, and the essence of the love between us. That is what lives on. We cannot accompany them on the journey. We can only learn to let go of our loved one, again and again, with every breath they take. With each solitary journey home.

MAKE AN ACT OF POWER

No one ever told us we had to study our lives, make of our lives a study, as if learning natural history or music, that we should begin with the simple exercises first and slowly go on trying the hard ones, practicing till the strength and accuracy became one with the daring to leap into transcendence. . . .

ADRIENNE RICH

Sometimes it's called prayer. Sometimes it's called magic. Sometimes it's called an act of power.

Now you're probably not crossing worlds or engaging in astral projection as you sleep. You're probably not manifesting a cure for cancer or a winning lottery ticket either. (Although you never know.) There's such a lot of hype out there along with the nuts-and-bolts advice of changing your life one step at a time. Not just within what is popularly called the New Age movement, but within what I call creative consciousness.

Alas, I am no master of consciousness, creative or otherwise. Or else all the excess weight of all the years would magically disappear from my somewhat sedentary posterior. But along with the outrageous claims of the new millennium, there is some good advice floating around out there. I call it practical spirituality.

I have learned many things from practical spirituality. What I learned in a lifetime of sorting out the wheat from the chaff is that there is a commonality among various religions and philosophical movements around the world. They have at their core a reverence for the earth and an acceptance of the brotherhood and the sisterhood of human beings. They have at their core a basic unity and a divine order that can be translated well into daily life. Along the way, I've discovered a technique or two to bring spirituality down to earth and into useful practices. Practical spirituality.

One of the things you do in practical spirituality is to make an act of power. You need to make an act of power when you are tired of waiting for your life to change for the better. You need to make an act of power when you're in a rut and digging deeper every day. You need to make an act of power when you've been hurting for a long time and don't know how to make the hurt go away.

If everything is composed of energy in the universe, from stars and trees to carrots and cornflakes, then you are composed of energy too. By making an act of power you can learn to change the energy in whatever situation, problem, emotion, or relationship that you are bogged down in.

An act of power is simply a conscious change that you make, not just in your thinking, although it starts there, but in measurable, quantifiable ways that teach your mind/body/emotions that such a change is possible, probable, and doable. Maybe an act of power for your body is getting up an hour earlier and getting out the door on a morning walk— move that body!—and saying as you do it, "This is an act of power that I do for the good of my body." That's a simple example. Maybe an act of power lies in creating. Creating something wonderful and precious and uniquely yours—a collage, a mask, a painting, a poem—and saying to yourself, "This is an act of power that I do for me. This is a creative act of power that enhances my life." Maybe it's about going back to school at whatever age you are. (Even if you will be older than the professors. That's okay. They'll respect you more.) Maybe an act of power lies in taking the first step to starting your own business or revitalizing your current one. Maybe an act of power is selling everything you own to travel all over the world unencumbered for a year, before settling in a sunny spot. But let's start small, shall we? Acts of power don't have to be gigantic.

Sometimes it has to do with relationships. Forgiveness, anyone? Old family dynamics that need to be changed. Standing up for yourself. Showing up for yourself. Taking care of yourself and others in new fresh ways. Changing the energy.

All these years of learning and growing and becoming wise. Don't you know enough now to make an act of power? To choose your own life, your own interests, your own concerns, your own path? To choose what you want to do for the rest of your life? Who you want to be with? How you want to spend your time?

Begin now. Make an act of power, however small. Seize the day. Reclaim your life. And then make another act of power the next day and the next. Until you get what you want. Until you become all that you are. Until you become the power. The empowered woman.

Remember, it's all just energy. And so are you.

CONCLUSION: OWNING YOUR LIFE

You need to claim the events of your life to make yourself yours. When you truly possess all you have been and done, which may take some time, you are fierce with reality.

The words I write on paper tell me how to be a woman. Years later, I will read a passage and remember that I was taught through those words and through the expression of the ideas within the passage I wrote, just what I need to know and remember.

When the woman in my novel *Families* realizes the strength and the power of her passage through her life, the mistakes made and the lessons learned and the loves of her life lost but not forgotten, she goes to a place in the park near her home on her sixtieth birthday and begins her accustomed, solitary run.

She is startled to encounter along the path a woman about twenty years younger than she, who is, as she comes to find out, the woman she once was. Past and future meet in the present moment. The older woman is then able to help her younger self continue onward with her life. More, she is able to see the pattern of her own life as a great woven tapestry of time and events.

You own your own life. You, and only you, are responsible for the authentic woman that you become as you live your life with grace and courage. You are Body Blessed, Mind Radiant, Emotions Passionate, and Spirit Strengthened by all that you have experienced, all that you have learned, all that you have become. It is, after all, a journey of discovery. How do you find the thread that leads you to the pattern? By reflection, by contemplation, by living fully and wisely. And by telling your own story.

For it is in the telling of our lives that we discover who we are. And know it all to have been worthwhile, this journey that arches in a great circle from birth to death, this thread of life that winds us down all the days, this winding circle that unspools past, present, future so that our lives are the pattern of womanhood that we have woven, the warp and the woof, the width and the depth. The tapestry of our lives.

This luminous fabric of who we truly are in our entirety enfolds and strengthens us for our continuing journey.

What happened at the end of the story? I'll tell you. The mature woman, the authentic woman, the aware, reflective, compassionate, self-realized woman, after helping her younger self, just keeps right on moving. I have the idea that this happens, again and again, in more than books. And as the wiser woman goes forward under the green cathedral of the trees, she realizes this: "I have found my hero and she is me. And I continue. I endure."

As do you, dear friend. As do you.